/ P O N D

R I V E R

O C E A N

R A I N /

FIND PEACE IN THE STORMS OF LIFE

CHARLES LATTIMORE HOWARD

Abingdon Press
Nashville

POND RIVER OCEAN RAIN
FIND PEACE IN THE STORMS OF LIFE

Copyright © 2016 by Abingdon Press

All rights reserved.

Library of Congress Cataloging-in-Publication Data has been requested.

ISBN 978-1-5018-3103-4

16 17 18 19 20 21 22 23—10 9 8 7 6 5 4 3 2 1
MANUFACTURED IN THE UNITED STATES OF AMERICA

Contents

Preface

nao mitashi hana / ni ake yuku / kami no kao

How I long to see
among dawn flowers,
the face of God

Matsuo Bashō

This little book could have been written differently. In fact it originally was. *Pond River Ocean Rain* was at first a compilation of devotional and theologically inspired poetry. Scribbled poems free of grammatical rules and free to dance on the pages of my journal as if no one but my eyes and God's eyes were watching. That is how I see the world. A beautiful dancing poem, reflecting Truth[1] at a "slant," to borrow a word from Emily Dickinson.[2]

A simpler and perhaps more direct version of this text might have been called *Stillness, Trust, Mystery, Movement*. In the pond that

---

The Japanese portions of the haikus you see at the beginning of each chapter are from Matsuo Bashō and Sam Hamill, *Narrow Road to the Interior* (Boston: Shambhala, 1991). The English translations are my own.

is just a few minutes from my office, I hear words of stillness, of peace, and of the call to be set apart. Sitting by the mighty river that winds near my home, I read words of trust and of deep submission upon the light flowing currents. When I visit the shore and the ocean just an hour's drive away, I learn of mystery, I learn of smallness and greatness, and I learn of love. And from time to time, when the rain comes down, I see humility, growth, and how movements develop—one drop at a time.

My poetry was about the poetry all around me. I was attempting to make sense of my own journey with and to God. At some point in the writing process, I felt led to move from poetry to prose and to move from a theopoetic journal to what I pray is a small text that is more accessible and that is a blessing to others.

And that's what this book is meant to be. A blessing. I have been blessed in the writing of it. It has offered me an opportunity to look into the water and see if there might be something within that I might draw out and share with others. It has given me an opportunity to pause and look within my own journey. There is grace in telling stories. Vulnerability and risk for sure, but most certainly there is grace in the telling and in the listening.

I pray that this is grace for you. What follows are several short reflections. Read them one at a time or all together. Whatever feels right for you. This was not written all at once. It found its way to the page like the rain finds its way to the city where I live. There were some days where much was written. And then there were dry spells of waiting. Some seasons where day after day saw literary precipitation. And other seasons where there was drought. The reading of the book might be the same.

Preface

When writing, one is often asked for whom one is writing. Who is the target audience? That's a difficult question for me to answer in some ways. I have been blessed by many books for which I doubt I was the intended reader. Some books have just found their way to my hands and I am thankful that they did. Maybe this book could be that for someone.

And yet, this book is also written for anyone on the journey of life who desires to draw closer to God. Some are just beginning to consider responding to God's call of love in their lives. Others may have been aware of their walk with God for much longer. I pray that this be a blessing wherever one is along the path.

I have sought to keep this intentionally short. Words are beautiful and dangerous things. In his song "Submerge" the singer Maxwell, whose music has always moved and inspired me, sang that "words are demeaning . . . they can't describe."[3] When daring to utter something of God, it is wise to tread very carefully. Whenever I reread Barbara Brown Taylor's *When God Is Silent* I find myself reminded that we often say too much with too little care when speaking of the Divine.[4] Within the Book of Job, after pages and pages of attempted explanation of the "why" of God by the book's namesake (along with his wife and his friends), God breaks through what seemed like an unlistening silence to ask, "Who is this that darkens council by words without knowledge?" (Job 38:2 ESV).

It is best not to say too much when it comes to matters of the Spirit. And yet we can never come close to saying enough in regards to the depth and majesty and beauty and goodness of God. Never too much and never too little. It is best to tread carefully and reverently.

Preface

At the end of each chapter, you will find a few questions to sit with. The book is short, but your time with each question need not be. These aren't easy questions. The best ones seldom are. Whether you engage these questions as an individual or as a part of a group, I pray that the Spirit leads you to new depths. That actually was my original title for this project, "New Depths." Writing it has certainly taken me to new places; I pray the same for you.

The best books in my library have drawn and, in rereads, continue to draw me closer to God. This quite simply is my prayer here. I hope and pray that you may grow closer to God in the reading of this small offering. That is the only reason I have written it and the only reason that I share it.

I am an expert of nothing. Please do not see me as any kind of wise old spiritual guide. I have a muddy path of mistakes and missteps in my wake. Many more mistakes lie ahead I'm sure. Rather, I hope that you see me or, better yet, this book as a fellow sojourner. Walking with you. Perhaps you'll glean something from what I have been shown.

One final word. I consider it a profound honor that you are reading this. I have been blessed over the years to have been published in a number of spaces, and to this day I find myself sincerely surprised that anyone takes the time to read what I have written. What a gift you give me in reading this book. I pray that you can feel my deep gratitude. May this be a blessing for you.

Pond

furuike ya / kawazu tobikomu / mizu no oto

> The old silent pond
>   a frog dares to jump into
>   the sound of water.
>
>   *Matsuo Bashō*

The path is narrow and shaded by a whispering green canopy provided by strong oaks, willows, and pines. Its flora-lined walkway seems to invite those who walk slowly enough to breathe in the calm and wonder that emanates from these little fragile witnesses watching at their feet. The trust that these flowers have in reckless humans! The tender care of a graceful gardener or the slight step of a careless foot can mean the difference between a long beautiful season of bringing joy to others or an early winter of waiting for another chance.

Thank God we always get another chance.

The place to where this narrow path leads is a small pond—a Nazarene place, separate and set apart. But it is not far away; it is within. Separate within.

This pond is about a five-minute walk (two-minute run, but it's better to walk) from my office. The cacophonic cry of the city fills those minutes, and yet like so much of life today, I have been desensitized and hardly notice what is around me. I have been lulled to sleep by the loudest song.

The pond is in the midst of this. The trees around and, more important, the peace within it close out the noise of life and allow visitors to at last be quiet and truly hear. The pond gently invites those on the journey to stop running, to stop walking, and finally to be still.

The ancient philosopher Laozi is often quoted as saying, "The journey of a thousand miles begins with a single step." Differently translated it might read, "The journey of a thousand miles begins beneath one's feet."[1] I am drawn to the latter. That is closer to my experience, but I suppose it all depends on where one wants to go.

The journey into the world indeed begins with a simple step forward. The journey into the self may begin beneath our feet. Yet, the journey deeper into the Love of God, I believe, is best begun by being still. Like a pond.

It is that journey into and with the Love of God that this book is attempting to speak to. And the journey deeper into God's Love blesses and deepens our inward journeys into the self as well as our outward ones into the world. But the walk into the Great Ocean that is God must first pass by the Still Pond and the Great Flowing River.

~~ ~~ ~~

Questions to Hold

Do you have a quiet place to which you can retreat? If so, when was the last time you went there? Why is that place special to you?

If not, what would your ideal quiet place be? What's holding you back from going?

What journeys are you feeling called to take? A journey into yourself and your own heart? A journey deeper into relationship with God?

How might these spiritual or literal journeys help you connect with others in a richer, more selfless way?

Inaction sometimes is the greatest action we can take. Stillness is sometimes the most important move we can make. The beauty of this pond, the grace of its small yet active and fruitful ecosystem is based on its gentle stillness. If it moved itself into a roaring river or rose up and produced bounding waves like the ocean, the quiet turtles could not bask in the warmth of the sun in their daily peaceful adoration. The affectionate fish—in this pond they are koi—could not receive their gifted sustenance. Nor would I find this reminder to slow down amidst the constant speed and sound of the world that swirls around it.

Being still has been a necessary part of my walk. Stillness, I should add, is not for me the same as emptiness. While the waters of the pond might be still on the surface, there is much life moving within. Life is within. Love is within!

When I am still I do not empty myself. I would rather be filled with love than have nothing within. And being still allows for this to happen, or rather being still allows for you and I to notice that this has happened already. The love is there within us, even now.

Yet sometimes the waves of life rage so incessantly that it is difficult to see or feel that love.

Pausing and being still enough to notice love within and around is a deeply powerful and countercultural act. Stillness is a prophetic act. *Prophetic* is a fluid term that can move and be shaped in different ways depending on what or who is containing it. But the prophetic—the truly prophetic—can never truly be contained. The prophetic is wild. It is different. It is set apart—by God, God's love, and God's will. Thus, often it stands across the water from what the world is doing. In the case of most of contemporary society, stillness is a prophetic act, defying that which demands that we move quickly and move upward. It challenges the notion that it is better to be busy and occupied. It refuses the call to be constantly distracted and perpetually plugged in.

~ ~ ~

Questions to Hold

Can you think of a time when you were truly still?

Not just sleeping or relaxing, but still?

How did it make you feel? Why?

How might stillness affect those around you in powerful or perhaps prophetic ways?

Are there people in your life who need stillness?

Pond

As much as I love it there, most of my life has not been lived by the side of the pond. Instead, the image that comes to mind is of a crashing rainstorm. There is beauty in the storm, in the bright lightning, the powerful thunder, the heavy rain that helps things grow. Storms, however, are not meant to be perpetual. God designed them to be temporary, brief moments in life, not a constant way of life.

Rain is a gift to a growing plant. And rain with strong wind can bring movement(s)! But too much rain can drown plants and flowers, rendering them unhealthy.

Far too many of us walk through life trying to weather storms with broken umbrellas. We live with a constant feeling of not-peace. For some, this is an aimless commotion or a tiring busyness from work. For others, it is a frightening chaos and lack of direction. By living in the storm, we miss the beauty, the peace, the joy, that peaceful Waters can bring. We miss seeing that we are not loved because of our survival in the storm, but we are loved just because we are ourselves. We miss that we are called and invited to do more than just hold on for a break in the clouds. There is more to life than this.

A slow read of the story of Jesus and His disciples being caught in the storm should invoke both awe and a hopeful gratitude. They ride not on a pond but on a sea, and while the disciples are busy working and fishing, the Nazarene is in a pond-like sleep.

The Gospel story relates that after a storm comes upon them, the disciples awaken Jesus, Who says to the storm (and perhaps indirectly to us and the storms that we create in all of our lives), "Quiet! Be still!" or "Peace! Be still!" depending on the translation. And the storm calms (Mark 4:39 NIV and ESV, respectively). No book explores this holy, chaos-and-fear-dispersing moment and what it might mean for us today better than Kirk Byron Jones's *Rest in the Storm*.[2] I have to give my former professor a special shout-out, not only because of the integral role he has played in my vocational life but also because the timeless truth that I found in that book is true for you as well. We don't have to go through life weathering not-peace. There is a stillness within and a Peace-Bringing Presence in the boat right next to you. Have faith.

⌒⌒ ⌒⌒ ⌒⌒

Questions to Hold

Think of a time in your life that you were "living in a storm." Who did you cry out for, and how did you resolve the turmoil in your life?

Is "storm" your normal state of being?

What is keeping you from asking the Peacegiver in the boat with you for help?

While I was in college, the clouds gathered in a way that I had difficulty seeing the Light. I nearly came undone from the swirling storm that I found myself walking through.

When I recount that painful moment in my life, I often tell others that I was "running too hard." With that phrase I am trying to convey that I was too busy and overstretched—that is, sprinting when I should have moved at a gently paced jog or, better yet, a patient walk. This running wasn't just my over involvement and my overcommitment. In hindsight, I was actually running from something. My deep grief. My constant insecurity.

There is a fine line between a healthy self-awareness and overly psychoanalyzing oneself. At the risk of crossing that line, the great formative event of my life was the loss of my parents. My being parentless in both great and painful ways made me who I am. Not having parents for my late teens and early twenties brought out two peculiar reactions from within me. On one hand, I sought love, affirmation, and attention, desperately wanting to fill the void left after burying my mother and father. On the other, I never wanted to let anyone get too close for fear that they would leave and break my heart too.

This was how my storm began. I had difficulty being alone, always needing to be surrounded by friends and always needing to be in a relationship. I got way too involved in too many clubs and causes while in school. And I certainly believed in the things that I found myself drawn to, but there were moments during which my motivation was my need to be loved. That fuel can drive you to make some unhealthy decisions. It caused me to take on responsibilities that I did not have the time for. It led me to invest my energy into my clubs and activities rather than into my academic work. Predictably, my grades began to suffer. After the fall semester of my junior year, I was placed on academic probation, and then after the following spring (a season in which I missed more classes than ever before), I was kicked out of school.

Things began to go south with the person whom I was dating at the time. And my rudderless ship spun further off course after a bad internship in the field that I really wanted to work in. The pain and embarrassment were amplified at the thought that I was letting my deceased parents down. Parents who I every single day wished were there for me to call and get some advice from. Or go home to. Or get a hug from. Instead of running to them, I ran to alcohol and drowned my grief in beer. Often without my friends even knowing. A raging storm on my personal Sea of Galilee. Not peace.

And while my boat was sinking in the destructive hurricane that was my life, I did not once ask for help. I didn't let anyone close enough to know what was going on. Unlike the disciples who at least had the wisdom and humility to ask the Savior who was in the boat with them for saving, I thought that I could sail myself out of it.

Only after I received the letter telling me that I needed to leave campus—the cracking of the mast—did I finally turn to God.

I went to the pond on my campus—the same one that I wrote of earlier. I prayed with a desperation that I have rarely felt. While in prayer there, through my shame and loneliness, somehow God's love got through. Amidst all of my shortcomings, my literal failures, my hidden addiction, I knew and felt that I was still loved. The storm in my heart was calmed, and my boat floated at peace. Cracked for sure, but not sunk.

I felt led to reach out for help from certain faculty and staff members, and over the next several weeks God used them to help me get back in. A few retaken exams and rewritten papers later, I was once again enrolled without missing any time. And it would be that September of my senior year that I would also stop drinking and smoking and finally hear and respond to the calling God had on my life. And just to show how good God is, just a few months later, I met my beloved future wife.

I can't say that I was fully healed from the wounds and insecurities of my life, but I began the healing process. My ship had—and indeed still has—cracks in it, but it was no longer sinking.

The clouds parted and I finally saw Light.

~~ ~~ ~~

Questions to Hold

How do you deal with the stress of "running"? In healthy ways or unhealthy ones?

Are you running *to* or running *from*?

To what? From what?

Have you ever asked the One in the boat of life with you to bring peace to your journey? Why not?

Stillness allows for that which is hidden within to come to the surface and teach. I walk to the pond near my office not to escape but to find. And it is life that I find there. Beautiful living friends. Among them my favorite animal, the turtle.

Seeing the turtles gather on the log in the middle of the water reminds me of the need to slow down, the need to take my time while walking, the need to sometimes be still. I watch as my shelled friends stretch their necks upward toward the sun, listening to Something or Someone with ears that only an upwardly aimed stillness can bring. All the while soaking in the warmth from above. Stillness allows us to be warmed by the light of the sun.

It is difficult for me to articulate why I love these creatures so. Perhaps it is the way they seem to take their time, never rushing, taking in everything that comes across their path. The elders use to tell me to remember that "Jesus did a lot of things, but He never ran."

There's so much to love about these little slow-movers. Maybe I love them because their homes (their shells) are always with them, whether they are climbing warm moss-covered rocks, wading through cool muddy banks, or diving into dark unknown depths. A whispered reminder about always keeping our loved ones close even when on the move.

Turtles are walking ponds, and we can be too. Moving slower than everyone around us. Slow enough to bring home with us. Slow enough to be a pond in the midst of a busy city.

There is a reason why giant tortoises are among the longest living creatures: "The race is not to the swift / or the battle to the strong" (Ecclesiastes 9:11). I can hear scripture whispering to us. This is the opposite of the message that so much of the world screams: "The race" is won by those who work the hardest and run the fastest. But so many of us are running on the wrong track. Let's take a break and come sit by the water. There, perhaps, we can see clearly which race we are really called to be in.

Along with the turtles this still pond is home to the large koi who swim beneath the water. These silently majestic fish, often called "giant gold fish," never want for food, with daily visitors dropping crumbs into the water. *Koi* is a Japanese word that means "love" or "affection." I smile at this and remember how loved I am. That I, too, have moments of waiting in Love like these submerged blessed ones, praying for some crumbs of wisdom, or peace, or grace to fall down. In the stillness we remember this. Love amid chaos. Grace amidst suffering. There is a trap that we fall into when running the wrong race. We think that our being loved (or liked or respected) depends on our performance. That if we don't run well, we won't be fed love. Koi know differently. Provision, attention, and light come no matter how hard they swim. And the same is true for us. If the love around us depends on our performance, then, it is not love at all. In the musical *Wicked*, the "wicked witch of the west" Elphaba sings: "Too long I've been afraid of losing love I guess I've lost. Well, if that's love it comes at much too high a cost."[3]

The truest love in our lives—from family and friends as well as Divine Love—comes without requirement. Meister Eckhart was known to speak of love *"Sunder Warumbe"*—that is, without a why.[4] That is how God and the best of our loved ones love us—that is, without a why. Just because.

During my most difficult vocational days, I retreat to the stillness there and sit with life. I am reminded of love. I remember that tomorrow is coming. I remember all that I forget while running. I learn how to smile again.

Consider my little teacher the turtle. There is a beautiful difference in the way that she moves on the land from the way that she moves in the pond. A gentle, restful slowness on the land. A free, playful gliding in the water.

The stillness allows for me to glide through the day with grace, unhurried, yet with a far greater ease than normal. For some time now, I have begun my days with a visit to the Pond. Only occasionally the pond near my office that my feet take me to. I mean the Real Pond that only my spirit can access. I want to stay there and remain still throughout my day, gliding along the way with a turtle-like freedom.

Beginning the journey of each day with the intentional act of stillness blesses each step that will follow in the upcoming hours. There are other animals outside of the water that seem to begin their day immediately working to gather food or to look for prey. Their earliest hours are spent in a self-serving toil. They work to survive. They busy themselves, while those within the stillness of the pond simply look upward, trusting and knowing that the Sender of the Light that is breaking through the canopy of trees above is the same One who will provide daily bread. So they don't scurry. They wait, or they playfully glide in peace.

From time to time the turtles come ashore on the banks of the pond and try to tell the squirrels about the Loving Light above. They whisper in slow words that the squirrels need not worry about the coming winter, because the same Love that brings bread to the koi is the same Love that shakes acorns from the trees. No need to run fast. No need to fear. Only a few squirrels have heard. The hearing ones have learned to glide through the air with a playful joy.

~~ ~~ ~~

Questions to Hold

Why do you think some people are in such a rush? Are you?

What might your day, your work, your ministry look like if you intentionally slowed down?

How are you reliant on God? For the big things and the small? How has that reliance been difficult or easy for you?

How do you begin your day? Think of ways that you can incorporate a quiet time or prayer time, be it morning, afternoon, or night. Take steps this week to spend time alone with God. Bring a journal and write down any words that God speaks to you as you spend time alone with Him.

I do not go to the Pond or to the River or to the Ocean or out into the summer Rain empty-handed. I always come while holding my cracked jar of clay so that I may dip it into the Living Water and carry it with me the rest of the day.

I come to fill it up. If I'm being honest, I am sometimes insecure about my broken jar. It is far from perfect. Cracked from my falling over and over again. It still holds Water, but the cracks promise to leak out whatever comes in. And yet I still come to fill it—to fill me.

What a dangerous misconception. That in order to visit Love, in order to visit the Water, we must have a perfect jar. What a sad mistake. That in order to journey with God we must be perfect. No, we visit the Water precisely because we are imperfect! And the stillness and peace of the Pond welcome us to its shores and into its depths with grace and love.

I submerge my jar into the Pond Water, beneath the surface where Love dwells. The Water flows through the opening in the top and through the cracks on the side. Submerged within the Pond there is a wholeness to my imperfection. Within the Pond, nothing escapes through my defects, but rather Love comes in through them. My wounds from losing loved ones, from my past of struggling with addiction, from my insecurity at almost failing out of college, or from my fears of not being a good enough dad or husband or writer or minister aren't blemishes or cracks that keep me from meeting God in the stillness. They are the exact spaces where God meets me with a healing and filling love. Love seeps in through the wounds.

When I pull my jar out and return to the path my jar is not fixed (and won't be until I leave it in the Pond for good). And though it remains cracked, I am reminded that it is not broken or at least not shattered. Sharon Thornton would remind us that it is "broken yet beloved,"[5] as we all are standing before God with the wounds of our lives.

And these cracks that were once an embarrassment to me are now in the loving service of the Pond. You see as I walk back along the path, the Water leaks out through the cracks of my jar, watering flowers along the way.

Henri Nouwen has been in my cloud of witnesses ever since my days of working in my seminary bookstore. His book *The Wounded Healer*[6] is one that I will always keep close. Its title offers a window into the great message held within. The wounds that we bear, very much like the wounds of Christ, can be used to heal others. What a redemptive message of hope! My suffering, your suffering, need not be in vain! And I see this nearly every day when students enter my office, unsure that tomorrow will come. When they are facing academic struggles or when they are wrestling with addiction or when they experience loss, sometimes God uses my wounds to allow for an understanding, compassion, and by His grace a healing love. I thank God that I am cracked but not shattered. Living Water is still within.

Questions to Hold

Think of a time when you were hard on yourself. Did you pull closer to Christ or further away? Consider the times when you made a mistake but were more gentle and forgave yourself. Was that more or less difficult than punishing your soul?

Are you aware of still being loved amid your brokenness? How might that awareness bring forgiveness toward others?

How might God use your wounds to heal others?

On busy days I take a break and walk to the pond. And as the sun moves from right above me to the side, beginning its afternoon descent, I see that it is time for me to head back to the office. I don't want to leave the Water and return to the path. My heart wants to stay there all day.

From time to time, rather than calling me to walk to the still pond, the *Love within the stillness* comes to me and I become undone. Light. Tears. Wordless worship. Received Love. Gratitude.

Julian of Norwich, the Anglican Saint, sings through the thin walls, "All shall be well. All shall be well and all manner of thing shall be well."[7]

When the Stillness visits us everything makes sense. Or it doesn't have to make sense. We become free from the very limiting need to understand mystery. This is where ponds become oceans!

I had moments like this when I was child. Moments in which everything just made sense. The word *peace* doesn't quite capture it. Everything was clear and there was within me a soul-knowing that "all shall be well." There was not only nothing to worry about but also a closeness to God that communicated a clear love. It was something like a butterfly landing on your face.

The Pond walks (has already walked) the path and It comes to us. If we are still, it might alight upon us. And sometimes even when we are not still, but need to be, it graciously comes. Then we are no longer at the edge of the pond. We are both far away and submerged beneath the surface. We become free.

And I do not want it to end. I grieve when the tide subsides. I walk away with face and clothing still wet from being soaked from swimming and from playing in the peaceful pond. The Water is still on me and in me. I still carry it in my leaky fragile jar of clay.

~~ ~~ ~~

Questions to Hold

When do you feel ecstatic—that is, pulled out of yourself?

What fogs your vision from seeing that "all shall be well"?

Ponds are different. Apart. They do not find the need to connect with other bodies of water. Needless of a creek or stream plugging them in to others. They are separate and free. And that takes courage.

It is far easier to be a part of a larger body. To run with the currents. But the Pond presents a different calling: "Come out from them" (2 Corinthians 6:17). It whispers: "Do not conform to the pattern of this world" (Romans 12:2). It calls: Be different. Be odd. Be a pond in this desert. Be away from the polluted waters that all of the great boats prefer.

This is one of the most overlooked messages within the world's major religions, this model and calling to be different. Within my own faith, we are followers of Jesus the Nazarene. The root word of Nazareth is the Hebrew *nazir*, which can mean "separate branch" or "set apart." Jesus has become so domesticated (and the *Dominus* should never be domesticated) in contemporary Western society that we can miss His radical, very different, wild life and message. How odd He was in His time and how very contrary His message is to a world overrun by violence, greed, and selfishness.

Within Judaism, this not only is often the message of the prophets (calling us to be different from the powerful majority) but also was the witness of Moses to the point where he physically left the center of power and went apart. There he met and heard from God.

Or take the prophet Muhammad who drew a people out from the power centers of his day to start something very different, calling people to "submit to God" (the meaning of Islam) rather than to their own desires. Or the Buddha who also left and became set apart from the wealth, sheltering, and power of his upbringing in order to find enlightenment and freedom. Or consider these words about having the courage to be different, composed by my very favorite of Indian poets, Mirabai. So enamored by the divine, she finds herself dancing gleefully:

> Mira dances, how can her ankle bells not dance?
> "Mira is insane," strangers say that.[8]

Oh that we had more brave souls who are not afraid to be the only ones dancing while all others stand. I love how her family describes Mira as being mad, when it is they who are mad. How can one not dance in the face of such beauty? In the glow of such love? Standing still is madness. If only more of us had the courage to be dancing ponds wanting to soak the world, rather than muddied puddles.

~ ~ ~

Questions to Hold

What might being set apart vocationally look like in your life?

Consider and journal different ways that you might be brave enough to be "mad" for God like Mirabai. How can you act on these actions this week and the next? Put a plan in motion to be "mad" for God.

Pond

Swimming in the pond is hard. Not dangerous, but hard in a different way. Once when visiting the pond near my vocational home I met one of the pond's caretakers. She was employed to take care of the little turtles, koi, and other creatures. Her work was lonely. At times it was messy as she knelt on the muddy banks. It certainly was thankless unlike the degreed oceanographers or the ship captains of the sea. She only hears the quiet gratitude of creatures whose language is peace. I saw the way that people looked at her as she got in the pond. "How gross!" I imagine some of them thought as she entered into water that is not sterilized with chlorine. "And how disgusting to share water with those creatures." Most of us prefer to swim in lonely pools with chemicals that burn our eyes. It's hard to see after swimming in pools.

Serving and loving and living at the Pond is difficult. As a child, after learning of the concept of evaporation I wondered how the pond remained full. Oceans and seas and the bay near the home I grew up in constantly filled each other, but this pond...from where or by Whom was it filled?

This is a question that those called to be "set-apart ponds" must ask with trepidation. When we are called to be different than the deserts that we live in, how do we get filled? It is of course by the Rain Water from above. And the scientists remind us that the water coming down from the clouds above is from the water in the rivers and oceans that sent it up from elsewhere. Indeed, because of the water cycle (the hydrological cycle), the ponds are in fact connected and never alone. And neither am I. Neither are you.

I am an orphan. Until Heaven I will remain physically apart

from my parents. Aloneness and loneliness have been my gift and pain throughout my life. I need solitude, and yet I fear it. I love the quiet of the morning when no one else in my home is awake, and yet I weep when my wife and daughters are away. I am slow in allowing others into my heart because of a fear that they, too, will leave, and yet I deeply need that connection.

I am a pond. Apart from the waters that once poured into me. And yet I remain connected to them. They still rain down onto me. I still evaporate up toward them.

I am a pond. Blessed by my separateness, calling others to be separate as well. Blessed by stillness, yet so much is moving beneath the surface. Blessed to be connected via the heavens to all the water around me.

The pond calls us to this. To be still. To be separate. To be subtly connected to the rest of the water in the world.

We need more ponds in the world—more individuals who will dip their jars into the great Pond. Souls who will walk through the day unafraid to be different. Free enough to walk slowly while others are rushing. Brave enough to "be still and know" while others move and climb. Broken enough to share their water as they walk the path of life returning from stillness and walking with stillness.

You know ponds are the one body of water that almost all of us can make ourselves. Oh how beautiful our gardens, our schools, and our workplaces might be if we knelt down and began to dig. And then let it be filled with Living Water. I pray for more pond makers and individuals who are brave enough to enter into the graceful stillness of the Pond, like the young woman who cares for the turtles and koi at my pond.

~ ~ ~

Questions to Hold

From what clouds are you filled?

What changes must you make in your life to become a pond maker or pond caretaker?

River

araumi ya / sado ni yokotau / amanogawa

The sea is rough, yet
over all, even Sado
flows Heaven's River

Matsuo Bashō

It carries us away. Outside of the cities we live in. Outside of ourselves. That is actually the definition of ecstasy: something that takes us outside of ourselves. The world needs more ecstatic people who live beyond themselves.

This river is ecstatic. And with jumping in we risk everything. We risk losing ourselves. We risk not coming back. We risk sinking to the bottom. We risk allowing the Current[1] to guide us rather than being guided by our own feet on the banks.

From time to time I sit on the banks of the river that runs through my city. Those who first walked this land and those who first swam this river named it *Toolpay Hanna*, which in the language of the Lenape means "Turtle River."[2] Ah, turtles live in ponds and rivers—oceans too. Thank God they are everywhere!

When the river was (re)discovered by the exploring Dutch, they named it the *Schuylkill* River, which means "Hidden River."

There is a Hidden River that carries us away. Protective and free and grace-filled like the turtle. The walk to this body of water is slightly longer from my desk, but I find my way to its banks. And sit. And dream. And imagine what it would be like to jump in. I'm a good swimmer. I'd be fine. But that isn't going deeper. I want more than just a brief dip in the waters.

Faith is jumping in and letting the Current take me where It wants. Submitting to the Wind and the Living Water and the "Ground beneath it all," as Paul Tillich might call it.[3] We (seem to) control our steps and our direction when journeying on the ground. Journeying in the River where the strong Current moves us, where the direction laid out by the River guides us toward our destination, is a very different path—one that calls for a deep trust and a deeper faith.

It's dangerous. There are painful rocks beneath the surface that we might strike a foot on. We might be bitten by something that dwells within. We might go over the waterfall. We might not come back out of the River. Traveling by River was never promised to be easy, but it is indeed holy. Submitting the direction of our lives to the Current is one of the most difficult endeavors we can undertake. But the walker who wants to go deeper must indeed jump in. With it comes love unimaginable.

And while trusting and allowing the Current to guide us brings life and love, there is a cost. That cost is the forfeiture of our perceived control.

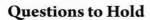

Questions to Hold

What makes you ecstatic? Both excited ecstatic and also "coming out of oneself" ecstatic?

What's holding you back from jumping into the life that you sense the Current would like to lead you to? What can you do to overcome that fear?

I first contemplated this notion of not being in control during my season as a hospital chaplain. I did not enter seminary with the intent of going into chaplaincy. All students were required to complete something called C.P.E., which I would later find out stood for Clinical Pastoral Education, a phrase that didn't clarify what was in store for me much more than the three abbreviated letters. C.P.E. is an internship experience during which seminarians are asked to serve as ministers in what is usually a non-congregational setting. And for me that setting was a hospital in West Philadelphia.

I suppose I should pause and attempt to define what a chaplain is and does before I continue with the story about C.P.E. It is telling, in a sense, that I am asked from time to time by my students, "What exactly is a chaplain?" I often reply, only half joking, that "I'm still trying to figure that out!" If forced to offer a definition, though, I might say that a chaplain is a clergyperson or spiritual leader serving outside of a congregation, usually as a part of a team. Chaplains are perhaps best known for their roles in the military or maybe in hospitals or even prisons. Many professional sports teams have chaplains. In the United States both houses of Congress have long had a chaplain. And many colleges and universities have chaplains.

The particular role of a chaplain, of course, differs from situation to situation. Some chaplains preside over services and various types of gatherings while others emphasize counseling more than ceremonial service. Still other chaplaincies revolve around programming and education. We describe our chaplaincy at Penn as having three particular facets. We like to say that we are the "heart of religious life," meaning that we "oversee" and journey with more than fifty different campus ministries. The parallel that I like to use is that we are similar to an athletic director. She does not coach each sport, but she works to make sure that each team is thriving and that their players are growing as student athletes. Similarly, I do not serve as the campus rabbi or priest or imam. Nor am I the campus minister to one of our Protestant Christian groups. We are blessed with several amazing men and women through whom God works powerfully. And while I'm not one of the campus ministers, I work to make sure that they have everything they need, to advocate on their behalf, and to help to grow their ministries, by God's grace.

Along with overseeing religious life, we are a part of the crisis response and counseling team at the university. When tragedy strikes, we, along with student intervention services, public safety, and our counseling office, reach out to affected students and community members. And from time to time, I am tasked with making the call that no parent ever wants to receive to tell them that their greatest fear has come true. This is by far the most challenging part of chaplaincy.

Finally, the chaplain has ceremonial duties. I like to tell students that I will bless them on the way in at the opening ceremony and I will bless them on the way out at graduation. I would not be the university chaplain that I am without the time that I had as a hospital chaplain.

In ways not unlike physicians and nurses, the chaplains of the hospital where I did C.P.E. are assigned a floor or a specialty field, and there they "take on" a certain number of patients. During that first summer I was assigned the neurology floor, and every day I would make my rounds, checking the charts of each patient that I was visiting and then adding to that chart after our conversations. We were a part of the care team (along with the doctors, nurses, social workers, and surrounding families). Some cared for the bodies of the patients; we cared for their hearts, minds, and spirits.

Along with our responsibilities to the floors we were assigned, each of the five C.P.E. chaplain interns was asked to spend one overnight on call in the hospital. This entailed us sleeping in the office and responding to the needs of the entire hospital, including the emergency room and trauma bay whenever we might be called upon throughout the night.

On their first overnight shift, young chaplain interns are given the opportunity to shadow a veteran chaplain. I had just turned twenty-three years old. A year before I was living in a frat house and finishing up college, and now I was visiting hospital patients, baptizing babies, and giving last rites. In reflection, I think that I was probably a little young to be involved in an intense hospital chaplaincy like that one, but on that very first night on call, I had no idea what I was getting into.

The gentleman that I was shadowing was a Lutheran pastor who felt called to chaplaincy. He was nearly forty and had been at the hospital for two years. I remember the anxiety I felt when the rest of the chaplaincy department left at the end of the work day leaving the two of us to keep watch over the whole hospital.

We began by making rounds on each of the floors, checking in with each department's head nurse to see if there were any patients they thought could use a visit. These cold-call visits brought us in touch with people who were awaiting surgery, recovering from surgery, being treated for heart trouble, waiting to deliver a baby, and more. About two hours in, the on-call pager went off. We were called up to the room of a man who was afraid because of his pending surgery. I kept quiet while the more experienced chaplain listened and tried to be present with all that the man was feeling. In the midst of our prayer we were called to the labor and delivery floor where we were asked to pray for a prematurely born little girl. We left there to respond to a page for a woman who was dying. Her family wanted prayer for her transition. Nearly out of breath after racing up the stairs and down the hall, we arrived at a room holding more people than it was designed to. The African American family surrounding the bed could have been my own. And the aged saint covered in white sheets might have been one of my grandmothers. She had a stillness known only to those who are just minutes from seeing God.

After some brief introductions we held hands in a circle and my mentor chaplain offered a prayer commending her soul to God "from whence she came." While we were still in prayer, the machines signaled to us that she had passed away.

After hugs, gratitude, and condolences, my teaching chaplain and I left the room. Standing by the elevator, he asked how that was for me. He must have seen the tears on my face. I replied that "It was beautiful and painful. Awe-filled and scary. And if I'm being honest, it pushed a few of my buttons with my mom and my dad both passing aw—." I didn't even finish my thought before the pager went off again, alerting us to the fact that a trauma patient was on the way to the hospital.

With speed, we made our way down the stairs and through various shortcuts that I would later use on future on-call nights. When coming the back way to the emergency room there was a long hallway whose walls were painted with a slightly out-of-place mural of a light blue sky. The sky in the mural is filled with butterflies and birds and flowers and very peaceful signs of nature.

While walking this long hallway, reeling from the chaotic pace of an evening that would not even permit me a moment to process my feelings, I flippantly said, "Man, this is out of control." The chaplain stopped and turned to me and said something that I have never forgotten.

"Not being in control is a part of the discipline."

It takes a Pond-inspired discipline to be able to ride the sometimes wild uncontrollable Current of the River. I do not claim to totally be at peace with it, but what that chaplain told me has proved to be wise counsel and an important challenge over the course of my ministry and life. I imagine many ministers and caregivers can relate. There is certainly a rhythm to ministry. Many traditions have annual holy days and weekly services that provide an important consistency to the vocation. For me, I move along an academic calendar that brings forth convocation at the beginning of the year, midterms, fall break, finals, and then winter break. We resume with the second semester, spring break, midterms again, finals once again, and then graduation before entering the much-welcomed summer recess. In late August, we start all over again.

And yet with ministry there are holy interruptions. Some are simply individuals dropping by the office because they need to talk.

They might interrupt sermon planning or some of the other quieter aspects of ministry and life. Other interruptions are more jarring, like the middle-of-the-night phone call alerting you to an accident.

If I may be completely forthright, over the years when I have found myself too often interrupted by the more serious kind, that is when I tend to explore other job possibilities quite simply because what I learned that first night of C.P.E. was true: ministry truly does have moments when it is out of control. I have been tempted to swim to the banks of this vocational river and climb out. But staying within the out-of-control-ness of ministry and the out-of-control-ness of life is an important discipline for us all to swim through.

～ ～ ～

Questions to Hold

When life feels out of control, what is your first reaction? Is that a healthy reaction?

Do you otherwise have a rhythm to your daily, weekly, or yearly life? How does it or how might it help?

The word *discipline* comes from the Latin word *Disciplina* meaning "teaching, instruction, or knowledge given." The Latin word *Discipule* means "one who is taught or a student." I have fond memories of entering my middle school Latin class and being greeted by my teacher who consistently said to us, "*Salve* (greetings) *Discipule*!" And our response was always, "*Salve Magister* (teacher or master)!"

This is much more of what disciplining should be—teaching. Sadly, the verb *discipline* has taken on a more punitive connotation over the years at the expense of the notion of instilling knowledge, wisdom, and instruction. Jesus called His followers Disciples (students to Him Who was called rabbi or teacher). This is a much better model of disciplining than spanking.

All parents at some point are confronted with the question of how they will discipline their children. I remember speaking with my former boss and longtime mentor/father/friend William about how he disciplined his daughters when they were younger. He said that he decided very early on that he would never spank his girls, because he did not want them to think that it was all right for a man to put his hands on a woman. There is so much in there about violence against women that I never forgot, but it also challenged my wife and me to consider disciplining our children in a way that teaches but doesn't punish.

A part of the discipline and teaching given to the one following after God is this very important lesson of not being in control. There is a discipline in swimming in wild waters rather than in safe pools. The wildness and out-of-control-ness of the River can be frightening and the fear of drowning can sometimes find its way into our minds. This inability to control a situation or a person often leads one to resort to violence in relationships. The lack of discipline around needing to be in control can lead individuals to make some terrible decisions. But it is important to stay the course of trusting and love. And to keep swimming and letting the Current be in control and not us.

Questions to Hold

What did discipline look like for you as a child?

How has it influenced the way that you see discipline today?

Do you have someone in your life that disciples or mentors you? What things have you learned that may allow you to disciple others?

S wimming in rivers is different than swimming in pools. The river is heading somewhere; the pool is not. The river pulls us. In the safe water of a backyard pool we make our own path.

Among the great privileges and benefits that I receive by working at a university, having access to the campus gym and the swimming pool within it is one that I cherish. When my schedule permits, I make my way to the pool just about every day. The pause in the intensity of the day coupled with the cooling of the water is felt grace. I go as much for the mental and emotional rest as I do for the exercise. It is also a time of embodied prayer for me. I love it.

I have also swum in the aforementioned river that runs near our campus. There the waters are untamed. They are free of the chlorine that burns eyes. In the river there is diverse life. The river itself is alive!

In biblical times there was a linguistic distinction made between "living waters" and other types of water. Water contained in a jar or a cup or a pool was considered not to be alive. Uncontained water in ponds, rivers, oceans, and in the rain is alive. Better to be free and living than to be contained, constricted, and unmoved.

To relate this to the human experience, there are voices that would caution against the untamed life. They would say that it is important to know where one is heading and how one is going to get there. I see this with some of my new students every year. At eighteen they know what they are going to study in school (they have already planned out their schedules for the next few years), exactly what they will do after graduation, what city they will live in, and when they'll get married, have children, and retire. There is something about looking ahead that is admirable and indeed important. But there is something tragic at not leaving room in life to be surprised—to be knocked over by a Living Water wave that might completely change everything in your life in an exciting new way.

Living with an openness to the wilds of the River is not easy, nor is it without risk. I have been a strong swimmer for most of my life. The fear of drowning never crosses my mind in a pool. I recognize it as a real possibility however when I swim in Living Water.

Questions to Hold

How would you describe a "safe" life, and would you consider your life to be, in some ways, too safe?

Are you living in contained water or Living Water?

What can you do today to break out of the "safe" life and live with the Living Water that cares for you?

I heard a pastor once ask his congregation if their lives were more like rivers or more like swamps. He explained that rivers, on the one hand, are places teeming with life within and around them. Historically people groups have often organized and developed cities and nations around them (Egypt and the Nile, Rome and the Tiber, London and the Thames). These rivers, the pastor went on to say, flow steadily between the riverbanks and remain ready to temper thirst, assist with cleanliness, help with travel, and offer food or even recreation. The river is there, consistently faithful with its calling.

Swamps, on the other hand, are messy. Rather than remaining within banks, they spread out over everything, making the land difficult to farm and nearly uninhabitable.

The pastor was making a point about being disciplined with our time and resources. Rather than doing too much and being spread out too thin (over everything like a swamp), we should remain disciplined and within healthy borders like a river. There is so much wisdom in this. Many of us, especially those who wish to help others and bring about positive change in our world, often have a hard time saying no. I see this with my best students each year. They arrive to campus with a number of interests and a number of gifts. They run for student government, join an a cappella singing group, become an after-school tutor at a local elementary school, join a fraternity or sorority, and get a job somewhere on campus, all the while taking six or seven classes. Some students find that this is too much and, once they see their first set of grades, realize that they were spread way too thin. But some students can actually sustain this thinly spread pace of life without seeing too many setbacks. Yet, what they miss is that they are only giving each organization just a portion of the best that they can offer. As present as they may attempt to be in the moment, they simply can't dedicate the time and attention that a class or an organization demands or truly deserves. Thus, they end up not giving their purest water but a muddied and at times swamped version of themselves.

That is not to say that rivers only serve one purpose. They offer drinking water, travel, fun, energy, and more. But they know their limits. They know that if they break out beyond their banks, they can become floods and become destructive to everything and everyone around them.

But what do we do if we find ourselves—our lives—being lived in a swamp. The first thing to do is to understand where we are. Swamps, by definition, are wetlands that have shallow waters in spaces called low-lying depressions. These depressions are spaces that have physically sunken below the surrounding areas. Being overly stretched and swamped can often lead to a burnout-induced depression that pulls us below those who surround us.

This shallowness only allows for a certain type of life to exist within rather than the full potential of vibrancy that a life in and by the river can bring. Once we realize where we are living—that is, a swamp—we can begin the process of reclaiming and transitioning the land.

Unhealthy wetlands can be reclaimed, experts say, by draining the excess water. This is hard to do as we often feel like we will go thirsty without the extracurricular excesses in our lives, but if we learn to say no, to rebuild boundaries, to move to the side of the river rather than the middle of the swamp, we can begin to live healthier, clearer lives.

Questions to Hold

In what way does your day-to-day life feel more like a river?

In what way does your day-to-day life feel more like a swamp?

What excess water can be drained from your life?

What can you do to be more like the Living Water on a day-to-day basis?

There are two types of drowning, I suppose: the bad kind that suffocates and the good one that allows us to finally breathe.

I have felt the bad kind before. Many of us have. That drowning, while walking around in the cruel land-river that is life. I have had seasons of life in which I simply swallowed too much of the polluted water that is busyness, stress, anxiety, and overwhelm.

Sometimes rivers and other bodies of water see whirlpools develop when storms arise. Life has whirlpools that we, from time to time, accidentally swim in. I have had my emotional lungs filled after having fallen into a whirlpool. There were too many emotions to name spinning me around and pulling me down.

Yet one of the lessons that I have been taught over and over in life is that "every night ends and morning always comes."

Two different seasons of my life have shown me this truth that I think is so very important for people to know. I have always loved sports. Playing, watching, coaching, or even just reading about sports have always grabbed my heart. I often find myself moved to tears when seeing individuals and teams give their all on the court or field or track. I love sports. But I can't say that I have always loved practice.

I have vivid memories of reluctantly making my way to the gym in high school to prepare for basketball or track practice. In basketball I was blessed to have been coached by a brilliant man who also taught me English in high school. We studied Dante during the day and a few hours later zone defense. He was the kind of coach who subtly but powerfully would sew life lessons into basketball moments; he was the best kind of coach. At the end of practice, he would line us all up on the baseline and select one player to come out and shoot two free throws. If he could make them, then practice was over. If he missed one, then we all had to run lines up and down the court (free-throw line and back, half-court and back, other free-throw line and back, and other baseline and back) as fast as we could. The point of this exercise was to create an environment that can simulate the pressure of shooting important free throws at the end of a long game so that if one is called upon to take a potentially game-tying or game-winning shot at the end of a real game, neither the pressure nor the fatigue will get to him.

I remember clearly one practice during which we watched our teammate make his way to the line where he confidently made the first shot (applause and grateful cheers from the rest of us) but missed the second shot.

"No problem. We all miss sometimes, man."

After running, we offered encouragement to our brother/teammate, "You got it this time, bro. Take ya time."

Another miss.

Sweating after this second round of running, we were a little more quiet but still encouraging.

Miss.

While we were breathing quite heavily after running our third set, our patience was wearing thin and the pressure began to mount for our teammate. It is when the eyes of others are really on you that you start to get the point of the drill. And as cruel and merciless as it was, it was not unlike the end-of-game moments that demand focus and endurance. But these drills also strengthen team bonds, compassion, and patience.

They also test faith. My younger fifteen-year-old self was tempted to think, *We are never gonna get home. We'll be running lines all night. This practice is never gonna end.* But the reality was that every night ends.

I learned this while running track as well. My track coach was another great man who played a fatherly role in my life. Once a week he would have us sprinters and jumpers do something called a "ladder workout" during which we would run 100 meters, then 200 meters, 300, 400, 500, 600, 700, and then 800 meters progressively and then work our way back down to 100 meters, each interval within a certain time goal. Describing this workout with words doesn't come close to capturing how brutal these practices were or how much we would dread them all day while in class. But, not only are these extremely good workouts for conditioning and speed, they also again taught me that even the worst of practices come to an end. Thank God!

My team sport days are far behind me now. Today I am more of a fan and coach, which are roles that I love just as much. But this lesson of every night ending is one that I continue to learn. As any parent will tell you, along with the great joys and adventures that raising children brings, it also brings some long, late nights. With each of my three girls, my wife and I had seasons of staying up with sick or teething or scared kids, trying to comfort them and get them back to sleep. And one can't help but look at the clock and see that it's only 1:00 a.m. and there is a full night ahead. During my evening prayers I often pray the following from the *Book of Common Prayer*, while keeping other parents and my old friends working overnight hospital shifts in mind:

Keep watch, dear Lord, with those who work, or watch, or weep this night, and give your angels charge over those who sleep. Tend the sick, Lord Christ; give rest to the weary, bless the dying, soothe the suffering, pity the afflicted, shield the joyous; and all for your love's sake. Amen.[4]

Life has taught me that every difficult night ends. And the light of morning always enters our windows. Every night ends. Every storm season of our lives ends, but how do we survive these long sad stretches?

I read once that one must swim diagonally to escape a riptide. There is hope in the diagonal. Different paths—away from the expected normal route. So many swimmers in life's rivers find themselves floating into dangerous riptides and end up being pulled in. There is another way. There are other currents—a Holy Current—that take us off the path most commonly taken.

For those of us who find ourselves in the midst of a riptide, we are called to swim diagonally. Cut across the downward spiral. Do not swim back the way you came. Nor should you continue to swim with the direction of the downward pull. Cut across it all diagonally. Keep your eyes on the shore. Climb out and then get into the River of Life. This River is also wild, yet there is a solid, faithful, steady Ground beneath it all.

~~ ~~ ~~

Questions to Hold

When in life have you felt as if you were in a whirlpool or an unending nighttime?

What might swimming diagonally look like for you?

The Nazarene was about thirty when He was baptized there. I was closer to thirty-four when I entered the chilly ancient waters of the Jordan River, though I had certainly heard of it. Paul Robeson's baritone and Jessye Norman's soprano both sang of the Jordan. My enslaved ancestors before that. That was how I first learned of the Jordan—as a child learning spirituals.

These songs in my head. Jesus in my heart. I held these as I entered that river. Visiting this land infused with holiness with other sisters and brothers in clergy, our tour brought us to the Jordan. And I asked to be rebaptized. All visitors desiring to enter the water are asked to shed their clothes and wear a new white garment. So much in the symbols. But more than symbols.

As I walked down to the banks I saw two creatures. I looked up and saw a dove. Not coming down from Heaven, but perched on a lamppost. Resting on the light. I looked down and saw a nutria—a creature also known as a river rat—swimming toward me. More than symbols.

I walked into the chilly waters trying to block out the tourists and the traps. A brother friend spoke ancient words and I went under. Wanting to stay there. Wanting to cross over. Wanting to hold my breath and sing spirituals underwater.

But the coming up again after submersion is more than a symbol too. The air was warmer than the Jordan. I felt clean. Old rivers can bring new life.

With peace above and filth in the water with me, I was somewhere in between. Neither dove nor rat. Whatever I am, I was accepted into that River.

This is a powerful notion discussed within the Talmud that explores the *yetzer tov* (our good inclination) and the *yetzer hara* (our evil inclination). The rabbinic discussion within this ancient text relates how God has given all humans both good and bad inclinations. All of us, no matter how righteous or pious or revered (in fact it says that it is often those seen as most righteous who are most susceptible to the evil inclinations), possess both.[5]

The tradition goes on to say that we should not try to escape or shed our *yetzer hara* because perhaps God has given it to us with a purpose. I would not claim to speak on Divine motivation around the creation of humanity, but I do think the Talmudic rabbis were onto something with this. I remember hearing a *d'var Torah* given by Rabbi Julie Schonfeld where she explained this tension. She suggested that each of us reach for and act upon our *yetzer tov* (good inclinations) while—in the teachings of Rav Amram—keeping the evil inclinations unrealized. But those evil inclinations, frustrating as they may be, play an important, sometimes not always realized, role in our lives.

Within the Christian tradition, we believe that the sacrifice made by Jesus atones for our sins, allowing us ultimately not to have to bear the punishment that our sins deserve, but to instead be found clean and acceptable in the presence of a perfect God in paradise. While that washing that we receive from Christ's death covers all that we have done and all that we will do, it does not mean that we won't sin again in this life. That potential for sin, or that *yetzer hara*, remains. It's a part of us.

When reflecting on my rebaptism in the Jordan, I contemplate that image of the rat and the dove before me and consider that perhaps I, and maybe all of us, have a little bit of both within. And that's OK. Because we are, as it says in Psalm 139:14, "fearfully and wonderfully made." And just as the river exists with all of the good and not so good within, God accepts and loves us with all of the good and not-so-good that's been a part of our stories.

Questions to Hold

How do you feel about your "not-so-good self"?

If there is a temptation to hate that part of you or that inclination within you, how might you gain compassion for yourself?

How do you think God sees you?

When looking at rivers, we only see the water. We often forget about the ground beneath the surface. When contemplating the ground at the bottom of the river, I remember theologian Paul Tillich's description of God as "the infinite and inexhaustible depth and ground of our being."[6] There is a floor that holds up all rivers. An unchanging base. And as the waters come and go, the ground remains there faithfully. And it is so with God.

This little book is full of metaphors, and all metaphors for God must be held loosely as they but dimly reflect the true image of God, falling as short as our best words. But they are good for the beginning of contemplation and the beginning of the loving glance from creation. Ground beneath the river is but another metaphor (as is the river itself) for what and how God is. God is steady though life flows on. And in some ways the goal of life—the goal of learning to jump in—is to sink to the bottom to the Ground.

Questions to Hold

What is the Ground at the bottom of your life?

Are you more focused on what's happening at the top of your river or at the Ground at the bottom of the river?

The goal of the inner journey with and to God is not simply to learn how to swim but rather to learn how to drown. The gifts of the Spirit and our time in prayer and meditation and worship and fellowship are sadly often thought of as tools for the journey, that is, things taught and learned so that we may avoid drowning in the waves of life.

Survival and endurance are fruits of the journey but not the point of it. For me as a Christian, I have certain scriptures that I turn to that remind me of God's grace, and I have "learned" how to pray and have found that actively worshiping God gets me through the difficult moments in my life. But my getting through the hard times in life is not the point of my religion or my relationship with God. Religion must be more than a life preserver or a crutch. This is one of the accusations that I hear about faith from students, that religion is, as Karl Marx said, "the sigh of the oppressed . . . the opium of the people."[7] And he was right—in part. Even a partial survey of the history of religious peoples demonstrates how faith and people of faith have contributed more to the world than just catharsis as evidenced by numerous social movements. This includes examples beyond the civil rights movement such as the efforts in India for liberation from English colonization, the antiapartheid movement (and many other movements), as well as the founding of a number of life-changing institutions such as schools, hospitals, and charitable organizations. Scholar Ram Cnaan's research has shed deep value on the role that faith organizations play in serving their communities outside of worship.[8] John DiIulio, the oft-cited professor and first director of the White House Office of Faith-Based and Community Initiatives, has also helped tell the story of not only the good news but also the great work of communities of faith in uplifting communities.[9] Marx missed the positive role that faith can play in changing the world and in changing lives in important, powerful ways. Yet he was right about how faith can become an opiate for some.

Opiates are used to dull the senses, permitting one to endure through pain. Religion can be an opiate of sorts, making one "dull" to suffering in the world by becoming so focused on the other world. And this focus on freedom and happiness in Heaven or paradise allows those who are suffering to "sigh" in the face of pain because they believe that while things might be hard now, things will be better after we die. So why fight for freedom?

I suppose the questions to hold will be: Is your faith an opiate blocking you from being present and feeling? Is your religion a life preserver disallowing you to drown into all that God has for you?

Drowning is the point. But what does drowning look like?

I use this metaphor very carefully because I actually almost drowned when I was a child growing up in Baltimore, Maryland, a lovely mid-Atlantic city right on the water.

Author and journalist James Spady would begin this narrative by using that famous phrase of his: "Wayblackmemories."[10]

A houseboat floating on orange sunset waters. Tied up yet free in the Chesapeake Bay. Low tide. Writing this I can't help but grieve at the fading images. Left over Afros. Baltimore. B More. They always wanted me to be more. No pressure, just hope and a lot of love. The boat was named Lady A, after my mother, Audrey. I never slept better than I did on that boat. Like Jesus in the storm. Again! Peace be still.

I must have been five or six. I spent the day crabbing. No big traps. No boat. Just me, a string, some leftover chicken (crabs will eat anything), and a net. I did very well that day.

I caught at least a dozen crabs (that's plenty for crab soup and some of my mom's crab cakes) and kept them in the white bucket that was their holding cell. I can't help but feel a breeze of sadness when I think of crabs. Thought of as the lowest class in the water. They are scavengers. Left out of schools and left to eat whatever falls to the bottom. Like turtles their home is on their back. Claws to fight and deter. Their weapons always ready like a restless knight in a castle already lost. Their drive to live and eat is far stronger than any notion of faithfulness or love. There is no sadder sight among sea creatures than watching crabs in a barrel. I wonder if they see themselves as so low. Perhaps we are all wrong. Maybe they actually quietly reign as kings and queens from the warm waters of the South to the Arctic where their long-legged brethren dwell.

On this warm day, I turned to walk back to our floating home in the light summer rain with my chest puffed out after my fresh catch. (I am surprised that I remember so vividly something that happened so many years ago.) Arriving at the dock after a long day of uplifting crabs, I attempted to make the step from pier to boat. A small gap between the pier and the boat that I had covered innumerable times was likely enlarged by waves coming in from the bay. I missed. I didn't know how to swim and began to sink to the bottom where I feared the remnant crabs might avenge their kinfolk that I netted earlier.

My father leaned over the side of the boat, reached in, put his big hands around my forearms, and lifted me up with ease. And after some tears and caring hugs, my mom cooked up the crabs and we feasted.

This story, long buried in my memories, would eventually work its way into a sermon that I once preached. It would be years later before I would see the parallel with how our Divine Father reaches down to pull us out of muddy waters as well.

～～ ～～ ～～

Questions to Hold

What is your faith (or how you're currently practicing it) not allowing you to feel and be present to?

Whose pain are you missing?

What might drowning look like in your life?

W hat is drowning? The losing of one's life. What is spiritual drowning? Allowing that life to be consumed by the Current. Allowing the Living Water to fill your lungs and take over everything inside of you. To fill all that is within. Thoughts, passions, loves, desires, dreams, hopes. To have it fill your life. And then to allow the desire to care for and love others drown out the desire to serve only yourself.

Meeting a drowned soul is a rare occurrence in life. But when you are embraced by one who has fully given his or her life over to God, allowing God to direct it however God wants, you never forget it.

Giving ourselves to God is different than believing in God. It is different than trying to please God. This is different than trusting in God for our salvation. This is forfeiting control and allowing God to guide.

This is not simply believing that there is a River that runs through our city. This is not just drinking from that River. This is jumping in and allowing the Waters to carry you to the next city where you can love, and serve, and carry out buckets of Water to the thirsty.

Jump in. And as the great musician Maxwell might say, "Let's drown deep" in Love.[11]

~~ ~~ ~~

Questions to Hold

Have you ever met a drowned soul?

How could you tell?

What would your life look like if you were fully drowned deep?

A Story: A Revision of a Tale from the Desert Fathers and Mothers

A young believer praying for help with her unbelief walked upstream with her teacher and asked: "Teacher, I pray by the shores of this river every day. I draw water from it to tend my garden. I wash my clothes on its banks regularly, and whenever I thirst I kneel down and drink. Now what more should I do?"

The teacher smiled and jumped in.

Years later the teacher returned to find the young believer had begun teaching her own students by the shores of the river. She taught them how to pray, how to draw water for their gardens, how to wash and drink as well. She even showed them how to jump in and swim.

Surprised to see her long lost teacher, the young—now older—believer said: "Teacher you have returned! I have taught my students just as you taught me, even to the point of jumping in and swimming."

The teacher replied: "I jumped in, but I did not swim."

Benedicta Ward, *The Sayings of the Desert Fathers: The Alphabetical Collection* (Collegeville, MN: Liturgical Press, 1984), 103.

Ocean

hatsuaki ya / umi mo aota no / hitomidori

Early autumn views
  the ocean and the rice field
    both are the same green

Matsuo Bashō

Heaven above kisses the water on a distant horizon that no vessel can reach. I feel the warm shifting ground beneath my feet. I'm led to remove my sandals. This is holy ground.

I breathe in deeply. The ocean air is fresh and dances above the water, dancing into all who wander close enough. And it is difficult not to wander close as the waters of the ocean seem to call me. Not just me, but all of us. Inviting us into its endless majesty. Here the water is not still. It does not wait for us but comes to us. Relentlessly.

The beach on the side of the ocean holds many visitors. My family and I come and set up safe spaces with towels or sheets or chairs to rest on. We allow the sun to warm us. To change us. My wife and I watch our children dig, build, run, and bravely play in water, a water that many adults stay away from. But the little ones go!

I have learned to love the beach though I feared it at first. As I have said before I use to prefer pools. Pools are safe. Tame. Not wild and unpredictable. But the ocean, with its wind and water in constant motion, is different. Real. Old, yet always new.

I walk down the hot sand of the beach with the bottom of my feet burning. It is almost enough pain for me to cry out. And I at last touch the cool water, going ankle deep but no more. This is a safe depth.

I can run away if I want to. Yet it is as if the Ocean continues to call me, beckoning me to come in and to go deeper. It reaches for me with each wave. Wave after wave after wave. The reach of this One that covers the entire earth. This One that makes up so much of who I am, keeps stretching forth to take hold of me. Embrace me.

~ ~ ~

Questions to Hold

How is God calling you?

If you don't perceive that, name some of the things and situations that might be blocking you from hearing that calling?

It reaches both day and night whether we are standing on the shore or not.

The Water reaches with a relentless love, never giving up on us, even if our fear drives us to run. This is how God loves us. Relentlessly. Like the waves of the ocean. The best marriages teach this in a small way. It seems that only moments had passed between our saying our vows on a rainy Saturday afternoon to us celebrating our ten-year anniversary in Paris. While walking around that beautiful city and reflecting on a decade of love, I remembered the many times when Lia hadn't given up on me. When she kept on loving me not only on the good days but through the bad ones. An unending love through grumpy moods, closed and buried emotions, long work days, pitiful male pride, and old wounds. She always stayed. I celebrated this love while in Paris (though I try to celebrate it every day).

On the Sunday of our anniversary trip we wandered old Parisian streets looking for a church to wander into. We found one that was meeting in a theater. The worship team sang a song in both French and English called "Relentless" by Hillsong United.[1] The simple refrain just repeats the line "Your love is relentless. Your love is relentless." Marital love at its best is but a small reflection of the large relentless love of God. A love that is not only relentless in that it never gives up on us, no matter what we do, but also relentlessly chases us. British poet Francis Thompson described this relentlessly loving God as "the Hound of Heaven" as it keeps chasing us like a benevolent hound running and running and running until it finally catches the object of its chase. Thank God.

I fled Him, down the nights and down the days;
I fled Him, down the arches of the years;
I fled Him, down the labyrinthine ways
Of my own mind; and in the midst of tears
I hid from Him, and under running laughter,
Up vistaed hopes I sped;
And shot, precipitated,
Adown Titanic glooms of chasmed fears,
From those strong Feet that followed, followed after.
But with unhurrying chase,
And unperturbèd pace,
Deliberate speed, majestic instancy,
They beat—and a Voice beat
More instant than the Feet—
"All things betray thee, who betrayest Me."[2]

Questions to Hold

How has God remained relentless to you over the course of your life?

What are some tough times and struggles that God has loved you through?

What might it look like for you—to borrow a phrase from pastor and author Tommy Tenny—to be a "God Chaser"?

Here is no thing, no one, no struggle, no mistake that could make God give up on us. A couple we met through church, named David and Nancy, have over the years mentored Lia and me. After church one day during a particularly low moment for me, they shared with me some wise words paraphrasing the brilliant author Philip Yancey.[3] They said that "there is nothing that can make God love you any more or love you any less."

Amen.

I have had moments in life in which I felt that what I had done was unforgivable. That I was unlovable. But the waves keep coming. The Water continues to call me in deeper so that the mud might be washed off.

My wife introduced me to the powerful and worshipful art of singer/songwriter Chris Tomlin. Tomlin wrote a song called "Indescribable" that beautifully speaks of this relentless love of God: "Incomparable, unchangeable. You see the depths of my heart and You love me the same."[4]

This love, this being known and yet still fully loved by an "Amazing God" is overwhelming, just like the ocean water is overwhelming. It is too much for many of us to take. It just doesn't make sense to some people. How can God love me—no matter what? How can I be loved when I don't earn it or don't deserve it? It seems too easy and quite literally "too good to be true."

Many children find it odd—appropriately so—that we have to pay for bottled water in a store, but the water of the ocean is free for all of us to play in, ride on, or drink when safe. It's baffling that we have to pay for this little bit in a bottle, but all of this great big ocean is free? Yes. So is God's love. And it is given to us generously. Consider the full passage from Philip Yancey referenced above:

> Grace means there is nothing we can do to make God love us more—no amount of spiritual calisthenics and renunciations, no amount of knowledge gained from seminaries and divinity schools, no amount of crusading on behalf of righteous causes. And grace means there is nothing we can do to make God love us less—no amount of racism or pride or pornography or adultery or even murder. Grace means that God already loves us as much as an infinite God can possibly love.[5]

~ ~ ~

Questions to Hold

Think of a time that you had difficulty accepting God's amazing love. Why was it so difficult?

Many believe that our earliest conceptions of God stem from our view of and relationships with our parents. Do you see any correlation in your own life?

If God loves in a relentless ocean-like way, how might you begin to love more like this in your relationships?

Ocean

The heat of the day and the heat of life at times have driven me to the water. And my soul's desire for a cooling respite occasionally emboldens me enough to run in. Feet first. Then ankles, then calves, next my scarred knees, and then I am halfway in. I walk deeper, feeling shells and seaweed below. I want to go deeper.

I pray that for you. That you will want to go deeper—in your relationship with God and with your loved ones as well as with those whom you do not yet love.

When I am awake, I follow my heart into new depths to play and to be moved. Pushed and pulled. Held by strong relentless waves. I want to be carried as I rest.

My heart listens to the ocean's lessons.

I watch for the Great Wave that approaches. Years ago, visiting the ocean, my brother-in-law Mark taught me how to ride the waves. Standing with great anticipation, I wait until it is upon me. Then I dive toward the shore, feeling the rush of water accelerate me back toward the sand. But then it pulls me back, inviting me to play again. To ride again. Joy! Joy! Joy! It is a wild game. Far more dangerous than a pool. Far more untamable and un-grasp-able. There is a risk. Courageous wave riders know that they might get hurt either by the rocks beneath or by the wild fish and crabs all around. I have had some rough moments during which I thought that the wave pushed me too hard. But I would not want tame waves.

When my daughters were little, after bath time we read through C. S. Lewis's *Chronicles of Narnia* together. In *The Lion, The Witch and the Wardrobe*, the character Susan asks Mr. Beaver about the mysterious Aslan whom she had been hearing about:

"Aslan is a lion—*the* Lion, the Great Lion." [said Mr. Beaver.]

"Ooh!" said Susan, "I'd thought he was a man. Is he—quite safe? I shall feel rather nervous about meeting a lion." . . .

"Safe?" said Mr. Beaver; . . . "Who said anything about safe? 'Course he isn't safe. But he's good."[6]

Playing and dancing and journeying with God should never be described as safe. God is wild and untamable. But He is also good. Wild like a lion. Wild like an ocean. It is not promised to be easy. Nor is it promised that we won't get hurt after getting in the Water. What I do know is that the Water is good.

Questions to Hold

Do you want to go deeper with God? Or are you content where you are?

Is this desire a dangerous form of spiritual ambition? Or is it more of a longing for Love?

And if you're feeling content, what has led to this spiritual plateau?

Have you allowed yourself to experience the wildness of God? What do you feel when you consider that?

The Water is deep. Diving off of my safe little boat, I break the surface and descend into darkness. This is not an evil darkness. Not all darknesses are created the same.

We are never too old to dive or sink to new depths. This is certainly a part of our purpose—that is, to journey further from the surface. All is not known down here in the dark of the Ocean. And that's all right.

It is difficult to see, and for some divers that is unsettling. Some who dare to jump in must have clarity lest they get out of the Water frustrated by the holy darkness. But there is a beauty in the mystery! Grace in the mystery.

The holy darkness of the Depths is light. As we swim deeper and deeper into the Abyss of Love the darkness of the space makes self-sight difficult. And that's all right too. Good even. For we dive not to see ourselves but to lose ourselves in the Depths. Or rather to be found.

In the Depths there is mystery. There is life, some of which remains unknown to marine biologists. Amazing that we humans who have walked this earth and observed these waters for thousands of years are still discovering new gifts of creation swimming and dancing in the mysterious darkness of the ocean. These nameless friends, I imagine, are undaunted by not being known. Humble teachers content with only their Creator knowing their name.

And I learn here. I want to know. I want questions answered. But I, by swimming in these Dark Depths, learn that some questions are only answered by mystery. And that's all right. We dive not for answers but for Love.

Questions to Hold

What if God called for you to live and serve within a hiding darkness?

Asked differently, might you be comfortable serving in a vocation that brings no acclaim, no praise, and no recognition?

What is an anonymous act of kindness that you might do?

To me the most awful (as in awe-filling) moment in the scriptures of my faith tradition is in the Book of Job where those who surround the book's namesake wade into the "why" in attempting to make sense of Job's suffering. Perhaps out of a desire to help Job (thinking that if the source of his suffering is known there might be a way to stop the "divine punishing") or from an insatiable desire to make sense of why Job suffered these tremendous personal losses, friend after friend tries to bring clarity to this incomprehensible situation. Even Job himself desires explanation and questions God about the great and enduring mystery of why bad things happen to good people. Toward the end of the book, however, God speaks and pronounces an oft-overlooked phrase that I have never forgotten: "Who is this that darkens counsel by words without knowledge?" (Job 38:2 ESV).

So much of what we know as humans, we know only "in part," to borrow from Paul of Tarsus (1 Corinthians 13:12). And that is all right. Seeking after knowledge is "all right"; in fact, I'd say that it is a powerful way to glorify and show love to God. One of the ways that my wife and I first loved each other was the desire to know more about each other. I am still learning! And yet I know that there will always be a part of my wife that remains a mystery.

Likewise, even more so with God. Seeking understanding about God is an act of love, an act of worship. Being at peace with the fact that God is above even our greatest thoughts is also an act of love and worship. Trying to contain God is dangerous and changes God into an idol. Idols can be controlled; God cannot. Once ocean water is placed into a container and taken back to shore, that water is no longer ocean. It is impossible to master the ocean. It is impossible to master God. It is impossible to know all things, to always be able to answer "why?"

I have felt this temptation. I have of course wondered why my parents died while I was so young. I can attempt to formulate an answer or a theory about how these events potentially changed the direction of my life. But I will never know the full answer, and that's all right. I don't need to know. I just need to know that I am loved. And I know that.

Each year my office couch holds several students who enter the difficult, but potentially strengthening, season of wrestling with what they believe. For some, this takes the form of discerning their position on a hot-button issue. For others, it may be wondering whether the Holy Scriptures that they grew up reading and learning are true or not: "How could all of those animals have lived together on an ark?" (Genesis 6:9–8:22). "How could Jonah have lived in the belly of a fish underwater for three days?" (Jonah 1–2).

My students often come looking for scientific proof or a clear definitive answer. And that I can seldom provide. What I do share, however, is that I, after all of the education that I have been blessed with, still believe those stories that I learned as a child. I believe that Noah built an ark with all of those animals. I believe that Jonah endured in the belly of the fish in the dark mysterious waters for three days. I believe that a man named Jesus lived, died, and came back to life.

I can't explain how. And you know what? I'm OK with that. I don't need to know how. I feel a peace with the mystery. It's not just that "this is what faith is—believing in the unseen," as many like to say. It's that this is a part of being a finite human. We can't know all. Finding peace with our humanity is an important part of life. Humans can hold a glass of water, but we cannot hold the ocean. I don't want to. If I could, it would cease being an ocean.

～～ ～～ ～～

Questions to Hold

In what areas of your life do you trust God? Professionally or educationally? As a provider? For eternal life?

How comfortable are you with unsurety? About the future? About your family? About scripture?

Have there been times in your life when you have had difficulty in letting God take control? What does control look like for you when it comes to your relationship with God?

Ocean

The ocean can seem so wild, mysterious, and unpredictable. How can we trust it? If I may diverge from the water motif, I'd like to turn to another majestic aspect of God's creation, to attempt to answer this question.

How many blessings are forfeited by not being open to conversations with those whom we are seated next to during air travel? My wife and I found ourselves visiting the beautiful state of Colorado on one of those partially work, partially vacation trips. Returning from this beautiful, mountainous land, we found ourselves serendipitously sitting next to a woman named Robyn. She had a very pleasant demeanor, with brown hair only partially tamed with a ponytail and attentive, listening eyes that betrayed a soul that finds joy in being a calm presence in the wild spaces of nature.

About an hour into our flight she revealed that she is a "trail psychologist." Having no clue what that meant I was drawn in. She went on to explain that she and her team work to restore and create the paths that hikers walk on their way up mountains.

I had no idea so much went into the laying out of our paths.

She went on to explain the careful intention that goes into constructing a path from the foot of a mountain all the way up to the summit. Paths, she said, recognizing the broader truth of her teaching, are intentionally designed at a certain grade or with a certain degree incline. One may think that the best way to the top would be a direct route going straight up. Yet, an experienced climber, or trail psychologist, would tell you that paths that lead straight up invite not only the quick onset of altitude sickness as well as the danger of falling but also the possibility of missing much of the mountain's beauty. Thus the journey is laid out in a gradual way so as to present a challenge, without overwhelming climbers, and in a way that they may enjoy the beauty of the climb.

She added that there is another important detail that she and her team always attend to. They work to the best of their ability to make sure that the path is laid out in such a way as to always keep the summit in sight. She explained that while climbers may not know exactly the path laid out before them, it is far easier to keep going when their goal, their inspiration, their hope, is still in sight.

Just a day before, Lia and I spent the day climbing up the famous Pikes Peak. Everything Robyn said was true. The incline up the mountain was enough for us to work up a sweat but not be overcome by the changes in altitude. Likewise, it did seem that we were being led by the path to various beautiful vistas, by peaceful lakes, and to colorful flowerbeds. And, as she said, the summit was ever in sight.

There is so much in there. Not least of which is the assuring notion that on most every hike or climb that we go on, someone has laid the path out for us already. What if that is true, as I believe it is, for our lives? What if there is a Divine Trail Psychologist or Divine Park Ranger who goes before us laying out our way? If that is so, then I think we need not worry about anything. I had a dear friend in college named Ishmael or "Ish," as we affectionately called him. Whenever I would share with Ish something that I was nervous about he would say, "Don't worry about it; it's already written, Doc!" Does this mean that we as humans have no agency, no free will to decide about anything? I can't say that I believe that. Of the theological question of whether we exist within a predestined framework or rather one in which we are given complete free will, I'm not sure. This is another one of those mysteries that I am comfortable with. Maybe we'll see it more clearly when we are on the other side. My hunch is that it is somewhere in the middle. The analogy I've used over the years with students is that we have a choice as to whether we want to get onboard God's train or not. And if we do hop on, God will drive us where He wants us to go. To bring it back to the mountain trail analogy, there is a path laid out on the mountain. Climbers are free, of course, to wander from the path. But some detours take us out of view of the great Summit. Other untrodden roads may be dangerous. But if we stay on the path laid out for us, we will certainly make it. I find comfort in knowing that there is Someone who knows all of the difficult climbs and the slippery valleys that lie ahead. And whether we are led up or down, as long as we keep our eyes upward on the Summit, we will find our way up to the Heavens.

This, sadly, is easy to forget. In some ways the greatest challenge in life is remembering who God is. Every morning I try to remind myself of this during my morning prayers when I read that famous passage from the Letter to the Philippians: "Do not be anxious about anything, but in every situation, by prayer and petition, with thanksgiving, present your requests to God. And the peace of God, which transcends all understanding, will guard your hearts and your minds in Christ Jesus" (Philippians 4:6-7).

If I may share one more brief story about the climb upward that our friend Robyn the trail psychologist shared with us. In Colorado, there are more than fifty different mountains that are taller than fourteen thousand feet. Some adventurous hikers take up the challenge of climbing all of these "fourteeners." At the top of each mountain, there is a register in which those who reach the summit can sign their name testifying to the fact that they made it.

One day, in the fresh mountain air, Robyn and her team were working to restore a trail when a hiker who had just reached the summit began to call out to them trying to get their attention.

"Are you all right?" she called to the man.

"Yes, but where is the register?" he yelled back.

Robyn told him that this particular mountain did not have a register. He responded by asking, "Then what was the point of my climb?"

The point she explained was all around him. It's the view from which you can see for hundreds of miles around. The point is the freshness of the air. The chance to see flora that only grows on top of the mountain. The chance to stand where very few have stood before. The joy of being on (with) the Summit. The point was the journey itself.

Reflecting on that story, I can't help but smile at the wisdom that this young trail psychologist/park ranger possessed. I realize that in this final section of this chapter on oceans, I have introduced a tangent of an already tangential story about paths on a mountain. But I just couldn't resist adding that second story about the point of the climb.

Playing and swimming in an ocean is very different than swimming in a pool. While doing laps in the pool on my campus, I often find myself glancing at the clock on the side of the pool, calculating my pace and gauging whether I'll beat my previous time. And as uncompetitive as I have become, when there is someone swimming next to me, I find myself sometimes trying to beat that person to the other end. Ah, the life of a former athlete.

When I am in an ocean, there is no clock to race against. There are no other swimmers heading toward the same wall that I am. I just swim and play while caught up in the majesty of the mighty Ocean that surrounds me. And that's enough. I don't need to win. I don't need to go faster. I just am. And the Ocean just is. A much better posture for life, I think. Thank you, Robyn!

Rain

kasa mo naki / ware o shigururu ka / ko wa nan to

The rain is starting
in the cold winter season?
Well, well, well, well, well.

Matsuo Bashō

The world was better without umbrellas. I don't know when or where it became a necessity for us to shield ourselves from the rain, to block the downward movement.

I hear dozens of mother and father figures reminding me that without my umbrella I could catch a cold. I know, I know. But the little boy in me still wants to run free and uncovered, with rain falling down onto my head and with water splashing up from the puddles that I absolutely must jump into.

Rain is different than ponds and rivers and oceans. Rain can fly. And we can too.

We can fly. We can fly, but we cannot become the Rain. We can only become one drop sent from the Great Cloud above down to the earth to make things grow. To fill up ponds and rivers and oceans.

Direction is important. Wisdom knows that things must come down in order to bring things up. When they were little, my daughters would approach me with open arms and raised eyebrows silently communicating their desire to be lifted up. To do so, I had to bend down to pick them up. And when speaking with children, the best teachers know that they must get on the children's level and kneel or sit on the floor with them. This occurs not only for practical purposes, allowing for better understanding with direct eye contact and a shorter distance for the sound of words to travel, but also for the powerful symbol communicated when one who is taller, stronger, and in authority gets down with those who are smaller, weaker, and under that authority. Coming down to the level of a child helps them grow up.

Rain knows this too. Crops cannot grow unless the water comes down to their level, even lower. The faithful farmer prays for rain during dry seasons, knowing that her sustenance and way of life depend upon Heaven opening the floodgates. God hears and sends a downward movement to replenish the land and bring growth. The rain comes down to the level of the crops and goes beneath it to enrich and refresh the land.

We are taught—or rather, so many of us have caught the commonly held belief—that in order to bring about change in our world, we must go upward riding such vehicles as power or money. We collect titles and degrees, climb political ladders, grow our bank accounts, and then through our influence and wealth we think that we can move individuals and people toward a goal or a new reality, thus creating a movement.

There is a difference, however, between pushing someone and moving him or her. When moving a heavy object from one place to the next, a mover may use a wheeled dolly. The dolly does not move the object. It is used by the mover of the object. When the dolly becomes the mover and not the human, the object is in danger of crashing because it is being moved and controlled by something without a heart. So it is with money and power. These are tools to be used by us, not lords that move and rule over us.

Thus movements are caused by the Spirit moving through people, and the Spirit leads us downward just like the rain.

Do not lead or push from the top; move from the bottom. Do not pull from the front; walk in the midst of your people.

～～ ～～ ～～

Questions to Hold

Have you been focused on the upward mobility of your career?

What might "going downward vocationally" look like?

What leadership style do you best respond to?

Which do you aspire to: from the top/front or from the midst of those you serve?

T he rain is humble. Compared to the ocean and other larger bodies of water, it is small. Sure, a rainstorm can span many miles, but each individual drop pales in comparison to the other water forms considered in this little book. In its humility, each drop does not need to be named like the great bodies of water around the world. They are at peace in their anonymity. Living their vocation without being marked on maps.

Movements and movement makers must be humble. When they seek to make a name for themselves it is no longer a movement but a campaign. A named ocean poured on top of a plant would not bring growth. It would drown and kill the crops. Nameless rain falling down onto and around and beneath vegetables will move them to grow.

This takes work and intentionality. One must be resolved not to let it be about them as others very often will try to celebrate an individual in the midst of the larger effort.

I will never forget a necklace that my old spiritual director M.M.C. used to wear. I shall withhold her name from this section as I imagine she would prefer it that way. During one of our sessions I remember looking at the cross that she was wearing and seeing the Latin phrase *Soli Deo Gloria* written on it. It means "To God be the glory" or rather "To God *alone* be the glory." When the farmer prays for the rain, she prays to God and she gives God thanks. The prayer is not to the rain, and the gratitude goes not to the rain but to the Sender of the rain. To the Rainsender alone be the glory. We are just droplets. We are not the Cloud.

Insecurity is a dangerous path that so many of us find ourselves walking down from time to time. This lack of security in our identities and in how we are seen often leads us to desire attention, affirmation, appreciation, and acknowledgment. We end up in this state for many reasons. Sometimes it is because we never felt affirmed while growing up. Or perhaps we don't receive appreciation professionally or in our family lives. Or maybe our harsh opinions of ourselves make us subconsciously desire the care and love of others to remedy our pained self-esteem.

Thus, we often desire the eyes and praise of those around us because it helps us feel better about ourselves. It's nice to be appreciated. Good bosses know how important this is. Healthy relationships find gratitude and affirmation flowing freely between two individuals in love.

And yet, the rain and M.M.C. (my old spiritual director) would say that God alone deserves the glory. It would be silly for me to take any credit for any good this little book might bring. On the earthly side, I was taught to read and write by my parents and siblings. I was blessed to have great teachers over the years. My job is such that I am afforded academic breaks during the calendar year so that I may write. Editors and friends have read through this manuscript helping to get it where it is. And Abingdon Press has been generous enough to publish it and help get it into stores and into your hands.

And it was God who brought me thus far. It was God who planted the idea to write this in my heart, God who gave the words, the experiences, the recall, this life. How could I take even a bit of the glory for this?

My sister use to enjoy telling me to "remember that you ain't nothin' but a worm!" For years I thought this was just sisterly teasing. But later she explained to me that she was trying to encourage me to be humble ('umble as she and other folks down South would say). I was, she told me, better off to remember that compared to our great big God, I was just a little worm. It is God doing all the heavy lifting in my life. And here is the beautiful thing: That great big God is concerned even with little worms like you and me. *Soli Deo Gloria*.

Something healthy happens when we direct the glory to God. It frees us. It allows us just to be raindrops. We don't have to perform. We don't have to be beautiful or brilliant or perfect. We also don't have to worry. We move in a trust that the Rainsender is keeping watch over the affairs of our lives. If God is to receive all of the credit, then God ultimately will carry all of the responsibility. The rain carries no worry as it flies to the soil. It soars with love. Knowing that it will soon carry out the Rainsender's will.

~ ~ ~

Questions to Hold

For whose glory are you working?

If you could make a major contribution to the world (such as find the cure for all types of cancers or make a discovery that could alleviate hunger) without anyone knowing that it was you, would you?

Dark clouds move in as silent harbingers of the coming storm movement. And it all begins with one drop. And then another and another. Moving and watering one by one.

Seeing a storm of peaceful demonstrators, our eyes witness them as one body. Yet there were thousands of individual decisions made that morning to gather and march and raise voices. Thousands of individual raindrops coming together to make one storm.

There is a common misconception, however, that alone these drops of water could not or would not accomplish anything. This is most certainly not the case. One drop of water sent on a downward mission from above can send ripples to the edges of a pond, moving everything within it. And so can you.

Don't be afraid to be the ripple starter. There are seasons during which our ponds are called to be still. And then there are seasons during which we must move others.

Often I am blessed to sit with friends and students who share with me beautiful and potentially impactful ideas. They share their vision and sometimes have even outlined how it will be implemented. But then something happens. Sometimes they hear a "no" or "not right now" in their spirit, and other times a different opportunity comes along. But many times people hesitate and put their ideas back on the shelf. They hesitate starting something new for fear that it will fail or that they will be embarrassed. And their dreams and visions evaporate before ever having a chance to make a ripple.

I have had individuals in my life that God has used to encourage me when my belief in myself or belief in a vision was waning. What a gift it is to have someone believe in you.

I don't know you, nor do I know what vision or dream you may be holding. But I do know the God who plants dreams in our hearts. And I believe in Him.

Why not try it? Why not dare to believe that something special might come from what you are holding? Perhaps you have been given this vision for "such a time as this."

Ancient scripture tells the story of the prophet Elijah who believed rain was coming although not seeing a cloud in sight. Kneeling atop Mount Carmel, he, with "his head between his knees," told his servant to go and look to the sea where he believed he might catch sight of a small rain cloud approaching (1 Kings 18:43-45).

Oh that we might see prophets looking to the Sea and praying for Rain today. So much of society today is in a drought. So many individuals are barely surviving while stringing together thirsty days and dry nights.

Which of us servants possesses enough hope to keep looking for a small cloud? To keep hoping for rain even in the face of a burning sun?

Questions to Hold

What ripples are you called to start?

To what storm might you join your single raindrop to?

What's holding you back?

What cloud of hope are you praying for?

Do you believe that it will come?

O ne of the blessings of my time in seminary was the opportunity I had to study Hebrew. For those who truly love reading scripture, I encourage you to read it in its original language, for, as cliché as it may sound, so much can be lost in translation.

On almost the first day of Hebrew class we explored the creation story in the original words it was written. I will never forget reading how *Adam* (man or human) was formed from the *Adamah* (ground, dust, or earth). The English words *man* and *ground* don't quite capture the connection between the human and the dust that God used to create him and us.

I was struck by a few things as I left Hebrew class that day so many years ago. I remember suddenly having a different emotional care for the earth that I was in some divine way connected to. I also remember thinking about how dust or earth alone is simply not enough to make a human. The Genesis narrative goes on to tell how God breathed His spirit into Adam, and then after that this new dusty and earthy creation could finally live (Genesis 2:7).

When I consider the ground, when I consider dust, I think of how nothing can grow with just dirt. It needs water from Heaven above to truly live. Just as the first human could not live as dirt alone, neither can we. We need to be watered by God's spirit to live. And there is put within us a natural reminder that dust can't bring forth life alone. We are given the gift of thirst.

As a minister I am given the sacred opportunity of being invited into the lives of many different people, and I have found that nearly all of us thirst. As a human, I have experienced this for myself. I don't simply mean the natural thirst for water that all humans have from time to time—for without water, we cannot live. I mean the heart thirst that we all feel. It is difficult to try to run the race that life is while thirsty. Why not stop and drink deeply from the Pond, from the River, or from the Ocean right next to us? Or better yet, why not lift up your head and let Living Water from Heaven rain deep into your heart. As Jesus said, "whoever drinks the water I give them will never thirst" (John 4:14).

While in high school, I loved running for our school's track and field team. I was slated as a sprinter and as a jumper. Much to my surprise, as I got older I grew fond of distance running. In my mid-thirties I began training for a half marathon.

The training schedule that I was following was designed to gradually build up one's endurance so that by race day, running the longer distance comes with stronger legs, lungs, and mental readiness.

The first week, the mileage was capped at two or three miles, and I would put on my sneakers, dash out of the house, and return back after hardly breaking a sweat and needing no water. As the mileage built up to four and five miles, I found myself drenched in sweat and thirsty upon my arrival back home. As my runs got longer, I noticed that I needed to bring water along for the journey or else I would not be able to make it back without walking or completely stopping. I was thankful for the little water bottle belts that might look silly but allowed me not to break stride.

My favorite summer run came one evening after my girls had gone to bed. For the first time, I was going to run ten miles. My path took me through the city down toward the river. The humidity of the air made me especially sweaty and thirsty, to the point where I finished my bottle of water by the time I reached the halfway point. It was dark, and I did not know if I'd be able to make it back home without walking. As I began to slow down, I felt a drop. And then another and another. Soon my shirt was soaked with sweat and rain, and I had to take it off. Flashing back to my childhood and shirtless, messy, muddy play dates with friends, I ran free through the downpour. Smiling at the natural refreshment from Heaven above. My miserable run became a joyous flight marked by the smile on my face and the delight in my heart. I made it home fine with a heart-thirst quenched.

That life-giving Rain is available for all of us. If we just keep our umbrellas down.

Questions to Hold

Is there an "umbrella" blocking you from God and from receiving all that God has for you?

What are you most thirsty for? What do you thirst for spiritually? Peace? Joy? Freedom? God?

From age eleven I lived full-time with my older sister Ami. Being only twenty-three herself, she was attempting to work, study special education in graduate school, and raise a quickly growing tween in Baltimore. In an effort to keep me out of trouble during the summer, she found a sleep-away summer camp that would get me out of town for ten weeks in June, July, and August. By God's grace and the generosity of the owners, I was given a full scholarship to attend this camp, which was all sports, all the time.

As amazing as it sounded, I was deeply nervous about attending. The camp was in a town called Naples, Maine. Being separated from my sister while still grieving the loss of my mother terrified me. But it was not only the distance that made me nervous. I quickly noticed that I was one of the only Black kids there.

The camp was called Skylemar and was predominantly Jewish. I arrived with a full duffle bag, a tear-soaked face, and major hesitations. Anti-Semitism was too big a word for me to understand back then, but I remember some of my family members speaking harshly about "those Jews" in nearby neighborhoods. Their cruelty was in response to racist or unfair business dealings and interpersonal relationships that they had with Jewish individuals over the years. This sad cycle of fear and prejudice was heavy on my mind as I sat in Shabbat services that first Friday. I stood out in the crowd of rowdy boys, not only because of my darker skin and different features or because of my Christian faith but because I was one of the few new kids. It's hard being the new kid.

However, instead of treating me with hate or neglect as I imagined, my bunkmates and the counselors showed me nothing but love and a care that provided a healing balm to a grieving boy. I remained a part of that community for ten years as a camper and as a counselor, learning both how to read Hebrew and how to love across borders, two things I might not have learned had I stayed at home during those pivotal summers of my life.

I have so many great memories of my summer seasons spent in Maine, but one of the best was what we would do when it rained.

The older campers stayed in bunks that surrounded a large natural grass-covered crater that we called "the bowl." It became common on warm rainy days in July to see teenage boys run shirtless out of their bunks to participate in what we called mud sliding. We would run as fast as we could toward the bowl and then dive on the ground, hurling down what became a muddy runway down into the midst of the bowl. It was disgusting and often painful when small rocks would pop up on the sliding path and scrape an unsuspecting mud-slider en route to the center of the bowl.

The spontaneous play was always made more fun when our counselors would join us in the messy game. They would dash and jump and slide much to the delight of a crowd of filthy, cheering kids who were so tickled that the older responsible folks would dare get in the mud with us.

Years later, while training for the ministry, this episode from my childhood came to my mind. In many ways—I came to understand—this is how God engages with us. We, over the course of our earthly journeys, find ourselves getting caught up and getting dirty in the mud of life.

The good news is that God doesn't leave us to wallow in the

mud on our own. Jesus comes down into the mud of life with us and loves us, even with all that stuff sticking to us. He helps us get out, get clean, and get back onto solid ground. And we don't have to climb our way out. He carries us.

This is difficult for many people to grasp. They think that we got ourselves into that mess, therefore we need to work to get ourselves out of it. At camp I learned that it is difficult to climb up a muddy incline by oneself. When a hand is offered, the path out is far easier.

In life we often think that we can get ourselves out of the messes that life brings. Twelve-step programs teach the great truth that it is truly only by God's help, strength, and love that we can, one day at a time, get clean. We can't unstick ourselves from addiction. But we "can do all this through Him who gives [us] strength" (Philippians 4:13).

We are loved so much by God that He reaches out to pick us up and carry us out. So many of us resist this and fight these Loving Arms off. Why not allow yourself to be loved? And carried? Let the Rainsender wash you off and set you back on the path.

Questions to Hold

Do you truly believe that God is *Immanuel*—God with us?

What muddy parts of your life would you like God to meet you in?

Consider praying and inviting God to come help you out of the muddy parts of your life.

"A love supreme. A love supreme. A love supreme." Three repeated words. The only lyrics to be heard on John Coltrane's subtly, yet powerfully, worshipful masterpiece bearing the same title. I long thought these were the only lyrics uttered during this classic jazz suite. The rest was said, sung, and whispered by Coltrane's saxophone and the other featured instruments.

Within the liner notes of "A Love Supreme," however, one will find words—a poem—written to the driving melody of the "Psalm" portion of "A Love Supreme." Reading these words while listening to Coltrane blow, Elvin Jones play percussion, McCoy Tyner bless the keys of the piano, and Jimmy Garrison move the bass is transcendent. The poem begins:

> A Love Supreme. I will do all I can to be worthy of Thee, O Lord.
> It all has to do with it. Thank You God.[1]

I remember the first time I read this poem. The phrase that stayed with me the most was "It all has to do with it."

My spiritual director M.M.C. use to say the same thing when I would come in and tell her three or four seemingly disparate stories about the happenings of my life since our last conversation. I might end my narrative to her by saying something like, "Sorry. I'm all over the place today," and she would reply, "It's all connected, Chaz. It all has to do with it."

It does all have to do with It. Psychologically and spiritually this is true in our lives as that which may seem compartmentalized in our day-to-day living most certainly intersects in important ways in our inner lives. But it all has do with It in another way.

Rain

Within this little book we have looked at four different water forms: ponds, rivers, oceans, and rain. I treated them separately, taking time to explore some of the lessons that each has to teach us. But the reality is that the distinct forms of water are connected in an important and enduring way.

Each year, children in their science classes learn about the water cycle (or the hydrological cycle). At the risk of oversimplifying a complex process, this is the ongoing movement and journey of water between various forms and "reservoirs." This is ice melting into a stream. A stream flowing into a river. A river flowing into an ocean. Water from the ocean evaporating up into the atmosphere. That water above returning to the surface of the earth as rain, snow, or other forms of precipitation, only to begin the cycle again.

It is profound to consider that the water that is on the earth today is essentially the same water that was here in the beginning. It just keeps dancing through the ongoing water cycle, bearing witness to the journeys of its human sisters and brothers over the millennia. It all has to do with it.

And it is amazing to think that though miles might separate them, small ponds are integrally connected to the large oceans and mighty rivers and to the rain that might be falling on the other side of the world. It's all connected. It all has to do with it.

And there is water in us. We, too, are a part of this beautiful water connection of all things. Francis of Assisi is right in referring to her as "Sister Water" as we are most certainly connected.[2]

This deep connection of all things changes everything for me. The Living Water flows through each of us. Every one of us. We are more than clay. More than *Adamah.* God's loving touch, spark, breath flows through each of us. The same Holy Breath (*Ruah*) of God animates each individual, giving us a deeply intimate connection. We all have to do with It, with God.

A true awareness of this must change how we engage with others who "have to do with It." How could we hurt anyone who has to do with It? How could we kill anyone who has to do with It? They have the same Living Water, Living *Ruah,* within them that we do.

One of the great tragedies of the human experience is our forgetting our connection to everyone around us. I love the great charge given to us by Jesus: to "Love the Lord your God with all your heart and with all your soul and with all your mind and with all your strength.... [And] love your neighbor as yourself" (Mark 12:30-31). Remembering my connection to others—to all others—allows me to love them as myself. The oneness amidst our differences is one of the recurring themes of the aforementioned writer and recording artist Maxwell's music. In "Lake by the Ocean," he writes:

> Can we swim a lake by the ocean?
> We'll be one like drops in slow motion.[3]

This is modeled best by the Triune God that I and other Christians worship. Again, words fall short of describing the relationship between God the Father, God the Son (Jesus), and God the Holy Spirit, but Christians believe that these three Beings live as One. Simultaneously three distinct Beings and One fully integrated God. This Trinity forms this perfect community where each is One with the other. Perfect community. Perfect Love. A Love Supreme.

Brother Coltrane got this. To see this, to live like this, is to live with a Love Supreme, *for* a Love Supreme. And a love like that can change everyone and everything that it is connected to.

Thank You, God.

~ ~ ~

Questions to Hold

How might tomorrow look different if you engage others as if they are connected to you as fellow children of God?

Can you imagine relating to your "enemies" differently when holding the notion of our "oneness"? What does that look like?

Can you imagine your amazing water-cycle-like love being contagious and starting a ripple-effect movement through those you are connected to?

David Greer: An Epilogue

Haru nare ya /Na mo naki yama no / Asagasumi

> Yes, the spring has come
> This morning a nameless hill
> Is shrouded in mist.

Matsuo Bashō

I find it difficult to imagine what the journey from the coasts of Western Africa to the docks of a young Charleston, South Carolina, must have been like in those late years of the 1700s. But my great-great-great-great grandfather made this treacherous journey—in chains.

His birth name is lost to history. As a young man he was captured and thrown onto a slave ship that sailed under either a Portuguese or Spanish or British flag. This is another unclear detail. Also lost to history.

On that journey, stripped of his name, he was now adorned with iron chains. Who else bore these shackles on previous journeys? More details and more lives lost.

He was likely chained to another man. His right leg chained to the left leg of another now nameless enslaved man. Once a beloved son, perhaps a husband, maybe a father. Now enslaved. And they would lie on hard wood thinly coated with hay as if they were animals in a barn. Rising once a day to walk a little. Fed leftover scraps of rice or yams or corn, just enough to survive the six weeks of their middle passage.

But history tells us that not everyone survived. Some died of starvation. Some from disease. Some were killed fighting for their freedom. And many others took their own lives choosing to fall into the mysterious waters of the Atlantic.

If given the chance, my first questions for my great-great-great-great grandfather might be: "Why didn't you give up? Why didn't you just jump?"

I imagine that he would say, "Because I never forgot where I came from. And I never forgot who I am."

Thirty or forty years later, a woman named Hannah would gather her grandchildren and tell them the story of what happened to the enslaved man who would later become her husband, their grandfather, and my ancestor. When he arrived in the colony, it was noticed that he had a mark on his chest. The mark, as it was told, was a symbol of Mandinka royalty. There was apparently a British law that forbid the enslavement of anyone with royal blood, and, with South Carolina being a British colony at that time, he was set free. That formerly enslaved but now free man would take the Anglo name David Greer, likely as a result of his connection with a Quaker family in the area with the surname Greer. And if they were like most Quakers of the time, they were against the institution of slavery. I imagine that they adopted the young "David" into their family and in doing so changed the course of an entire family's future. Ponds in a land dry for courageous stances for justice.

David would go on to meet and marry Hannah, and they would have a daughter named Sarah Greer. Sarah would have a daughter named Elizabeth. Elizabeth would have a daughter named Mary. Mary, my great-grandmother, bore the original Charles Howard, who would name his son, my father, Charles Jr. And my dad, known as Charlie, would pass on not only his name to my brother and me but also this story to us.

This tale of my ancestor born nearly two hundred years before I was born has always moved me ever since I heard it as a child. In one sense, it inspires me because had David Greer not been able to endure that long middle passage over the deadly waters of the Atlantic, I would not be here.

But there is more that he has given me. I am drawn into his long voyage over the waters. Waters he surely heard as they punished the wooden vessel that was coffin for some and sad bridge for others. I imagine the unsure future and destination tempted him to give up and lose hope. I imagine the calculated efforts at breaking apart families who spoke the same language almost made him forget his original tongue, his name, and who his parents were. I imagine the chains nearly made him forget that even with iron cast around his ankles and wrists, he was free.

I felt led to end this book with this painful but ultimately hope-filled story about a man's journey over the waters because I think that there is one final lesson within it. For many of us, the journey of life by, with, in, and over the waters has been and is a difficult one. Full of uncertainty and at times "in chains." Maybe not literally like David Greer's iron ones, but constricting nonetheless.

On that long deadly voyage over what would become a watery grave for countless others, something allowed him to hold on and endure until he finally found freedom. He never forgot where he came from, and he never forgot who he was. At this point history has forgotten his birth name, but he never did. The individuals on the ship, who likely beat him and treated him as if he were an animal, did not know who his father was, but he never forgot.

It is important that we never forget either.

This, I believe is the great trap of life: forgetting. We forget that God is all powerful. That God is loving. That with that strong and loving God on our side we have nothing to worry about. I remember this when I am caught up in ecstatic worship and drawn out of myself. I remember this when submerged deep in prayer, hidden in the waters of God's love. But when the stresses of life begin to pile up, it is easy to forget.

I love the image of David being marked on his chest. This was not only so that others might know who he was but also so that he would never forget.

This is what water has become for me. A reminder. A mark. So that I never forget who I am and Whose I am. Life may at times find me chained on a ship sailing toward unknown shores. But I can hear the Waters of the Mighty Ocean beating the walls of this boat, not to incite a fear within me, but to remind me that there is a power much larger all around.

The ocean spoke to my ancestor David Greer and spoke to him of freedom. May Living Water speak to you in the same way.

Acknowledgments

Inochi futatsu no / Naka ni ikitaru / Sakura kana

Between our two lives
there is also the life of
the cherry blossom.

Matsuo Bashō

In every season of my life, I have been blessed with wise and generous spiritual mentors who have held me in prayer, offered friendship, and provided wise counsel. Our relationships have been different with some being ongoing and constant while others were briefer and seasonal though no less impactful. It feels right to acknowledge the way God has used these beautiful souls in my life. That number includes Lavern Ball (Mimi), Ebenezer Afful, William Gipson, Sister M.M.C., Kirk Byron Jones, Larry Showalter, Debbie Little, Ralph Ciampa, Greg Brewer, Richard Morgan, Dennis Lloyd, Charles Bennison, Ron Sider, David and Nancy Filkin, John and Christine Fantuzzo, Steve Weed, Nipun Mehta, Anna Balfour, Stan Williams, Dave DeHuff, Kevin Bauder, Katie Day, Stephen Ray, Cornel West, Peter Gomes, Janet Cooper-Nelson, Jewelnel Davis,

121

Sharon Kugler, Deborah Blanks, Kenneth Clark, Alison Boden, Bruce Coriell, Susan Henry-Crowe, and my dear sisters and brothers in the Penn Religious Communities Council, The Ivy Chaplains Group, and in ACURA.

While I was a student in college and in graduate school, I held a number of jobs. I was an inept computer technician, a short order cook at a pizza place (fired for giving away too much food to my friends), a janitor, and a night watchman who was nearly sprayed by a family of skunks whenever I made my nightly rounds. But by far my favorite job was working in a bookstore while in seminary. I will forever be grateful to Joyce Simon, my boss-mom over the course of those three years. During calmer moments in the store, I would pull down interesting-looking books and read them at the counter while waiting for customers. I first met Francis of Assisi, Teresa of Avila, Catherine of Sienna, and the Beguines there. It was in the quiet of that store that I was first introduced to the writings of Henri Nouwen. Mary Oliver's poems first blessed my eyes and heart while standing at the counter. It was there that I read through Susan Howatch's Church of England series. I read my first liberation theology texts there along with books on spiritual direction, church history, mysticism, ecumenism, and various other faith traditions. It was there, surrounded by thousands of books, that I truly began to grasp the power words can have. Or rather, the way God's power can move through words. Thank you, Joyce, for allowing me entrance into that space and for your patience and grace to me over the years.

A book is too heavy for one person alone to carry. So many hands have aided the journey of this little book. Friends at Abingdon Press/ The United Methodist Publishing House, including Constance

Stella, Susan Salley, Debbie King, and Dawn Woods, have been kind and courageous in taking a risk on a project like this. Thank you! Thank you, Kirk Jones (again), for believing in this project and for helping it get seen. Christine Fantuzzo, Steve Kocher, Mary LeCates, Joe Loconte, and Daina Troy—who are family to me—read through versions of the manuscript and offered invaluable feedback. And many others have held this project in prayer over the duration of its writing. I remain grateful.

I have never known a day in my life where I did not know that I was loved, even after the passing of my parents. My three wonderful siblings made sure of that. My sister Ami stepped in and took on the full-time parenting duties. My sister Catherine Marie proved most generous to me over the years, sharing with me freely and believing in my various dreams. My cousin-turned-brother Joe showed me what it meant to be a responsible, loving man and has always been there for me. And my brother Chucky is the best man that I know, influencing my life perhaps more than anyone else.

Finally, I give thanks that I am privileged to journey with my beloved wife and best friend, Lia. Our first kiss was by the pond referenced in this book. And since that sweet afternoon we have walked by rivers, played in oceans, and danced in the rain. Always love. She is the best professor that I know, and I have learned so much from her. Much of this book flows from our conversations. Likewise, it's hard not to smile when thinking about my three daughters, Charissa Faith, Annalise Hope, and Evangeline Love— my own pond, river, and ocean. May you be clouds through which the rain comes.

Notes

Preface

1. I remember as a child learning to capitalize the word *God* when writing. Here, I use several different words when referencing God. *Truth* is certainly one of them, but also *Pond*, *River*, *Ocean*, and *Rain* as well. When a word is capitalized, the reader should presume that I mean God rather than simply a regular pond, river, ocean, or rainfall. To me these water forms can capture a portion of the nature of God in a way that human minds can partially fathom. Though it is important to remain in a posture of constant awareness that we cannot—certainly not on this side of Heaven if ever—come close to fully grasping God. Words and images will always fall short.

2. Emily Dickinson and Jackie Moore, "Tell All the Truth but Tell It Slant," in *Selected Poems* (Oxford: Oxford University Press, 2006), 40.

3. Maxwell, "Submerge: Til We Become the Sun" on *Embrya* (New York: Sony Music Entertainment, 1998).

4. Barbara Brown Taylor, *When God Is Silent* (Cambridge, MA: Cowley Publications, 1998).

Pond

1. Hua-Ching Ni, trans., *The Complete Works of Lao Tzu: Tao Teh Ching & Hua Hu Ching*, rev. ed. (Santa Monica, CA: Sevenstar Communications, 1995).

2. Kirk Byron Jones, *Rest in the Storm: Self-care Strategies for Clergy and Other Caregivers* (Valley Forge, PA: Judson, 2001).

3. Stephen Schwartz, "Defying Gravity" featured on *Wicked* (Original Broadway Cast Recording) (Decca Broadway, 2003).

4. Meister Eckhart, *Meister Eckhart: The Essential Sermons, Commentaries, Treatises and Defense* (Classics of Western Spirituality) (Mahwah, NJ: Paulist, 1981).

5. Sharon Thornton, *Broken yet Beloved* (St. Louis: Chalice, 2002).

6. Henri J. M. Nouwen, *The Wounded Healer: Ministry in Contemporary Society* (New York: Double Day, 1979).

7. James Walsh, trans., *The Revelations of Divine Love of Julian of Norwich* (St. Meinrad, IN: Abbey, 1975), 225.

8. Robert Bly and Jane Hirshfield, *Mirabai: Ecstatic Poems* (Boston: Beacon, 2004), 12.

River

1. Again, throughout this text, I use different water metaphors to describe God and the journey with God. Here the Current is a metaphor for Holy Spirit.

2. The Lenni-Lenape people lived in an area called Lenapehoking, which today is the eastern part of Pennsylvania and parts of Delaware and New Jersey. This wonderful group of women, men, and children deserve so much more than a footnote. But at the very least I though it important to acknowledge those who walked this space before I did if I'm going to reference it in this text.

3. Paul Tillich, *The Shaking of the Foundations* (New York: C. Scribner's Sons, 1948).

4. "A Collect for the Presence of Christ," The Book of Common Prayer, and Administration of the Sacraments and Other Rites and Ceremonies of the Church, According to the Use of the Protestant Episcopal Church in the United States of America (New York: Oxford University Press, 1945).

5. Emanuel Deutsch, *The Talmud* (Philadelphia: Jewish Publication Society of America, 1895).

6. Tillich, *Shaking of the Foundations*.

7. Karl Marx, *Critique of Hegel's "Philosophy of Right,"* trans. Annette Jolin and Joseph O'Malley (Cambridge: University of Cambridge, 1970), 131.

8. Ram A. Cnaan, with Stephanie C. Boddie, Femida Handy, Gaynor Yancey, and Richard Schneider, *The Invisible Caring Hand: American Congregations and the Provision of Welfare* (New York: New York University Press, 2002).

9. John J. DiIulio, *Godly Republic: A Centrist Civic Blueprint for America's Faith-based Future* (Berkeley, CA: University of California, 2007).

10. Spadey has begun many of his articles with this phrase. Much of his work can be found in *The Philadelphia New Observer* archives.

11. Maxwell, "Drowndeep: Hula" on *Embrya* (New York: Sony Music Entertainment, 1998).

Ocean

1. Matt Crocker and Joel Houston, "Relentless" on *Zion* by Hillsong United (Sydney, Australia: Hillsong Music; Brentwood, TN: Sparrow Records, 2013).

2. Francis Thompson, "The Hound of Heaven" in *The Complete Poems of Francis Thompson* (Brookfield, WI: First Rate Publishers, 2015), xcvii.

3. Philip Yancey, *What's So Amazing about Grace?* (Grand Rapids, MI: Zondervan, 1997), 41.

4. Chris Tomlin and David Crowder, "Indescribable" on *Arriving* (Brentwood, TN: Sparrow Records, 2005).

5. Yancey, *What's So Amazing about Grace?* 41.

6. C. S. Lewis and Pauline Baynes, *The Lion, the Witch, and the Wardrobe* (New York: HarperCollins, 1994), 79–80.

Rain

1. John Coltrane, *A Love Supreme* (Santa Monica, CA: Impulse! Records, 1965).

2. Francis of Assisi wrote in his "Canticle of the Sun": "Be praised, my Lord, through Sister Water; she is very useful, and humble, and precious, and pure."

3. Maxwell, "Lake by the Ocean" on *blackSUMMERS'night* (New York: Sony Music Entertainment, 2016).

Bibliography

Kojin no ato wo motome zu, kojin no motometaru tokoro wo motome yo.

Do not seek to follow in the footsteps of the wise; seek what they sought.

Matsuo Bashō

Bly, Robert, and Jane Hirshfield. *Mirabai: Ecstatic Poems.* Boston: Beacon, 2004.

The Book of Common Prayer, and Administration of the Sacraments and Other Rites and Ceremonies of the Church, According to the Use of the Protestant Episcopal Church in the United States of America. New York: Oxford University Press, 1945.

Cnaan, Ram A., with Stephanie C. Boddie, Femida Handy, Gaynor Yancey, and Richard Schneider. *The Invisible Caring Hand: American Congregations and the Provision of Welfare.* New York: New York University Press, 2002.

Deutsch, Emanuel. *The Talmud.* Philadelphia: Jewish Publication Society of America, 1895.

Bibliography

Dickinson, Emily, and Jackie Moore. *Selected Poems*. Oxford: Oxford University Press, 2006.

DiIulio, John J. *Godly Republic: A Centrist Civic Blueprint for America's Faith-based Future*. Berkeley: University of California, 2007.

Eckhart, Meister. *Meister Eckhart: The Essential Sermons, Commentaries, Treatises and Defense*. Classics of Western Spirituality. Translated by Bernard McGinn. Mahwah, NJ: Paulist Press, 1981.

Eckhart, Meister, and Josef Quint. *Meister Eckharts Buch Der Göttlichen Tröstung Und Von Dem Edlen Menschen (Liber "Benedictus")*. Berlin: De Gruyter, 1952.

Hua-Ching Ni, trans. *The Complete Works of Lao Tzu: Tao Teh Ching & Hua Hu Ching*. Revised edition. Santa Monica, CA: Sevenstar Communications, 1995.

Jones, Kirk Byron. *Addicted to Hurry: Spiritual Strategies for Slowing down*. Valley Forge, PA: Judson, 2003.

———. *Rest in the Storm: Self-care Strategies for Clergy and Other Caregivers*. Valley Forge, PA: Judson, 2001.

Lewis, C. S., and Pauline Baynes. *The Lion, the Witch, and the Wardrobe*. New York: HarperCollins, 1994.

Marx, Karl, and Joseph J. O'Malley. *Critique of Hegel's "Philosophy of Right."* Cambridge: University of Cambridge, 1970.

Matsuo Bashō and Sam Hamill. *Narrow Road to the Interior*. Boston: Shambhala, 1991.

Norwich, Julian, and James Walsh. *The Revelations of Divine Love of Julian of Norwich*. St. Meinrad, IN: Abbey, 1975.

Bibliography

Nouwen, Henri J. M. *The Wounded Healer: Ministry in Contemporary Society*. New York: Double Day, 1979.

Spady, James G., Samir Meghelli, and H. Samy Alim. *Tha Global Cipha: Hip Hop Culture and Consciousness*. Philadelphia: Black History Museum, 2006.

Taylor, Barbara Brown. *When God Is Silent*. Cambridge, MA: Cowley Publications, 1998.

Tenney, Tommy. *The God Chasers: My Soul Follows Hard after Thee*. Shippensburg, PA: Destiny Image, 1998.

Thompson, Francis. "The Hound of Heaven." First published in *Merrie England*, 1893.

Thornton, Sharon. *Broken yet Beloved*. St. Louis, MO: Chalice Press, 2002.

Tillich, Paul. *The Shaking of the Foundations*. New York: C. Scribner's Sons, 1948.

Ward, Benedicta. *The Sayings of the Desert Fathers: The Alphabetical Collection*. Collegeville, MN: Liturgical Press, 1984.

Yancey, Philip. *What's So Amazing about Grace?* Grand Rapids, MI: Zondervan, 1997.

Discography

Coltrane, John. *A Love Supreme*. Englewood Cliffs, NJ: Van Gelder Studios, 2002, compact disc. Originally released in 1965.

Crocker, Matt, and Joel Houston. "Relentless," on *Zion*. Recorded by Hillsong United. Sydney, Australia: Hillsong Music; Brentwood, TN: Sparrow Records, 2013, compact disc.

Maxwell. *blackSUMMERS'night*. New York: Sony Music Entertainment, 2016, compact disc.

———. *Embrya*. New York: Sony Music Entertainment, 1998, compact disc.

Robeson, Paul, Lawrence Brown, Ray Noble, Victor Young, and Jerome Kern. *A Lonesome Road*. ASV/Living Era, 1984, compact disc.

Schwartz, Stephen. "Defying Gravity" featured on *Wicked* (Original Broadway Cast Recording). Decca Broadway, 2003, compact disc.

Tomlin, Chris, and David Crowder. "Indescribable" on *Arriving*. Brentwood, TN: Sparrow Records, 2005, compact disc.

Praise for *Pond River Ocean Rain*

"*Pond River Ocean Rain* can be picked up throughout all the seasons of one's life. Charles (Chaz) Lattimore Howard has given us a feast for the spiritual imagination. Through deeply personal reflection and abundant metaphor he has created a devotional that is approachable, multifaceted, and genuinely hopeful. Whether we absorb it in one sitting or choose to pick it up periodically for smaller portions of succor to coat the soul, this little book offers a way to think about our own stories; to name our burdens, fears, or shortcomings; and learn to "swim" through them in a new way. It sets us free to let God hold us in the mystery of our lives. We need only to love." —**Sharon M. K. Kugler**, Yale University Chaplain

"For people of whatever religious faiths and of no religious faith, *Pond River Ocean Rain* will challenge the mind, stir the heart, and fill the soul. With words and images that are at once poetical and practical, Charles Howard gently guides the reader to seek and find deep truths and a kind of peace and joy that our noisy, busy, and at times brutal modern world seems built to deny us. It is must reading of a kind that can change and improve one's life for keeps." —**John DiIulio**, Professor of Politics, Religion, and Civil Society, University of Pennsylvania; Founding Director, White House Office of Faith-Based Initiatives

"Dr. Charles Howard is a rare breed: a public mystic who cherishes the social order as deeply as he does nature and the human heart. If you wish to know what that sounds and sings like, read this moving melody of a meaningful book." —**Kirk Byron Jones**, author of *The Jazz of Preaching, Fulfilled*, and *Refill*

"Charles Howard's marvelous new book is a refreshing drink of water for anyone thirsting for new ways to think about the presence of God in their lives. Through poems and poetic reflections, Howard invites us to imagine God through beautiful stories and provocative metaphors. By turns moving, playful, and inspiring, his book deserves a place on your shelf and in your heart." —**James Martin**, SJ, author of *Jesus: A Pilgrimage*

"This book has soul. At the same time, it is elegant and simple, practical and poetic, comforting and provocative. Chaz Howard invites you to find God in the stillness of a pond and the raging of an ocean. Drawing from the wells of wisdom across the generations, Chaz offers you a drink from such a diverse cloud of witnesses as Philip Yancey and Paul Tillich, Henri Nouwen and Barbara Brown Taylor, Francis of Assisi and Karl Marx, Chris Tomlin and John Coltrane. This is refreshing like a cold glass of water after a marathon. This book is like candy to the soul." —**Shane Claiborne**, author and activist, founder of Red Letter Christians and The Simple Way